Take
Care

Take Care

A Practical Guide for Helping Elders

ANN RHODES

HarperCollins*PublishersLtd*

TAKE CARE: A PRACTICAL GUIDE FOR HELPING ELDERS
Copyright © 1997 by Ann Rhodes.
All rights reserved. No part of this book may be used or reproduced
in any manner whatsoever without prior written permission
except in the case of brief quotations embodied in reviews.
For information address HarperCollins Publishers Ltd,
Suite 2900, Hazelton Lanes, 55 Avenue Road,
Toronto, Canada M5R 3L2.

http://www.harpercollins.com/canada

First edition

Canadian Cataloguing in Publication Data

Rhodes, Ann, 1932-
Take care : a practical guide for helping elders

ISBN 0-00-638491-9

1. Caregivers.   2. Aged - Home care.   3. Aged - Care.
4. Aged - Health and hygiene.   I. Title.

HV1451.R46 1997   649.8   C96-931883-9

97 98 99 ❖ HC 10 9 8 7 6 5 4 3 2 1

Printed and bound in the United States

Contents

Acknowledgements

First, I would like to thank all the caregivers, professional and familial, who took the time to give interviews and generally help furnish material for this book. I would also like to thank members of the health departments at all three levels of government—municipal, provincial, and federal—and members of numerous associations set up to assist elderly and/or disabled people for their help in giving interviews and supplying material.

Specifically, I would like to thank all the following people for giving generously of their time and expertise: Barbara Burns, social worker and consultant in gerontology, Ottawa; Floreen Cleary, executive director, Toronto branch, Victorian Order of Nurses; Jenny Evans, manager, Scarborough Health Department; Isabelle Everett, president, Gerontological Nurses Association, Hamilton; Dr. Michael Flynn, psychiatrist specializing in geriatric care, Nova Scotia Hospital, Dartmouth; Dr. Cyril Gryfe, internist geriatrician, North York General Hospital; Dr. Bob Hatfield, humor therapist, Foothills Hospital, Calgary; Dr. Pearl Karal, psychologist, Toronto; Bridget LeChat,

Canadian National School of Aromatherapy, Mississauga; David Loyst, music therapist, Riverside Hospital, Toronto; Gloria McIlveen, executive director, Alzheimer New Brunswick; Dr. H.M.R. Meier, geriatric psychiatrist, Wellesley Hospital, Toronto; Timothy Phillips, shiatsu therapist, Toronto; Ginny Schedewitz, regional manager, Comcare (Canada), London; Patsy Schell, executive director, Caregivers Association of B.C., Penticton; Dr. Ken Shonk, humor therapist, Grand River Hospital, Kitchener/Waterloo; Dr. Peter Singer, associate director, Centre for Bioethics, University of Toronto; Sorele Urman, director of coordinated client services, Baycrest Centre for Geriatric Care, Toronto; Dr. Wendy Yeomans, medical coordinator of the palliative care program, Vancouver Hospital and Health Sciences Centre; Sue Yerex, nurse, Westside Care Centre, Westbank, B.C.

I would also like to express my gratitude to HarperCollins editors Phyllis Bruce and Jill Lambert. Their comments and suggestions did much to improve my copy.

Finally, heartfelt thanks to Jerri Yeomans, my research colleague. This book is our third collaborative effort and, as always, she amassed a great volume of information and did a first-rate job of helping devise the structure of the book and constructively critiquing it, chapter by chapter.

Preface

As increasing numbers of Canadians are realizing, caring for elderly relatives and friends can be a demanding task. While acting as an informal caregiver to an elder can be satisfying, it can also be one of the hardest and loneliest experiences of a lifetime. In this book, I want to share with you the knowledge and wisdom imparted to me by professionals in the fields of geriatrics and gerontology and by lay people who have been, or still are, giving care to a family member or friend. In so doing, I hope to shed light on many aspects of informal caregiving, in order to help prepare you for the role of caregiver and to help make that role less demanding and more rewarding.

The need to disseminate information about familial or friendly caregiving for elderly people grows greater year by year. According to a report published by the National Advisory Council on Aging, some half a million Canadian elders already need substantial support, and of these 270,000—or more than half—still live in the community and need help from family members or friends. By the year 2031, the

NACA report states, the number of elders needing substantial support will have tripled, so if the proportion of those living in the community remains the same, some 810,000 people will need help from family members or friends.

Currently about 10% of the total Canadian population is over 65 years of age. Five years from now, in 2001, that percentage will have risen to 12, and by 2021 it will have risen to 17.

Nearly 80% of elder caregivers are women. And where there was once a tendency to describe these women as members of the Sandwich Generation, giving care simultaneously both to children and to one or more elders, the trend now is towards serial caregiving. In other words, a woman first cares for her children, then she cares for her parents or perhaps an aunt or an uncle, and finally, since she is highly likely to be younger than him, she cares for her husband. The reason for this change? Increased longevity. Where once you might have found a 45-year-old woman giving care to teenagers and a parent in his 60s, today you are more likely to find people in their 60s helping parents in their 80s.

Clearly, society must find ways of helping familial and friendly caregivers. Some caregivers will find they can't manage without some kind of help and will turn to professional, often institutional, caregivers. This will be extremely costly. To keep an elder in a permanent care facility can cost upward of $350 a day. Much of this cost is borne by provincial governments, which operate non-profit long-term care homes and subsidize residents who can't afford to pay, but, as is well known, provincial governments are already cutting corners wherever possible to reduce or avoid budgetary deficits.

Looking on the positive side, there are already some indications that caregivers will receive help. Indeed, some are already doing so. An increasing number of companies in Canada have programs providing help for employees who are elder caregivers. Among them are the Bank of Montreal, Caisses Desjardins, the Canadian Imperial Bank of Commerce, Manulife Financial and Union Gas. Some programs offer flexible work schedules and personal leave days for caregivers, or permit working at home. Others feature seminars and other means of imparting knowledge about caregiving. As well, some unions in this country now call for a given number of paid days off per year for elder caregiving activities.

Informal caregivers provide an extremely valuable service, and they will almost certainly be rewarded financially for this in the future. In some parts of the world (and in some parts of Canada) they are already being compensated. Norway and Sweden were in the forefront of the move to pay caregivers. Both countries pay salaries and have benefits and pension plans for them. Australia pays caregivers a small salary and has a "carer's pension," which is paid out to those who stop working in order to care for a significant other. England has a means-tested caregivers' allowance. South of the 49th parallel, more than 70% of American states pay caregivers who look after disabled elders at home.

In this country, Nova Scotia has a program to help low-income caregivers. The costs of the program are borne partly by the provincial government, partly by municipalities. Some municipalities have not yet agreed to participate in the program, so help is not available everywhere in the province.

In New Brunswick, care receivers are given money to purchase whatever services they need. However, they are not usually allowed to use the money to pay immediate family members. Quebec also gives money to the care receiver to buy whatever services are needed, no matter whether they are provided by professionals or by familial or friendly caregivers.

Saskatchewan pays familial or friendly caregivers if no one else is available to be a caregiver. This program considers caregivers to be employees and, as such, they may be required to care for other elders in the community.

Ontario is currently studying various options for making payments to caregivers. The provincial government has already enacted a bill making provision for payments to care receivers to buy services other than those provided by familial or friendly caregivers.

Will the practice of compensating caregivers ultimately be Canada-wide? Almost certainly. The costs of such programs are small indeed set against the costs of institutionalization, and governments must know full well that they will prove popular with the vast ranks of the baby boomers, some of whom are already taking on the caregiver role.

One Voice: The Canadian Seniors Network, an organization that lobbies for improved conditions for those aged 65 or more, is pushing for more help for caregivers. "One of the things we shall be pushing for is workplace family leave," Andrew Aitkens says. Aitkens, One Voice's director of research, elaborates: "This would broaden the concept of maternity leave so that people could also leave the workforce temporarily in order to look after an aging parent, relative, whatever." Such a plan would ideally see participants retain their full Canada Pension Plan benefits, and might even pay them the equivalent of Unemployment Insurance benefits, he says.

Another One Voice proposal is for a tax credit for caregivers. The user's tax return would show the number of hours spent in caregiving at a preset rate per hour, and this amount would be a tax credit.

By now you will have noticed the frequent use of the word "elder" in place of "senior." There are two reasons for this. Many older people heartily dislike the epithet "senior." As well, "elder" puts one in mind of "elders and betters," and many elders today are truly better people in some ways than we who came along later. They have experienced great social and political changes in their lifetimes that would probably have traumatized us. Many of them started life before the advent of aircraft, world wars, the nuclear age, television, and much more. They deserve our admiration—just as do those familial or friendly caregivers who freely choose to assume the burden of care and who dedicate themselves wholeheartedly to it.

CHAPTER ONE

Assessing Your Attitude and That of the Care Receiver

Sometimes, the partnership between a caregiver and a care receiver is a shining example of goodwill and dedicated affection. Consider, for instance, the case of 64-year-old Tom Pope, a retired banking executive living in North Surrey, B.C.

Tom has been a caregiver to his 60-year-old wife for about five years. She has Alzheimers, and her condition is deteriorating. She has not spoken for two years. "My driving force is that I love my wife and she loves me," Tom says. "She still knows me. For instance, today I was away most of the day, and when I came in she gave a little grunt. She was scolding me—like 'Where the hell have you been?' We have been married 40 years and I understand her body language.

"There are ups and downs," he continues. "There are times when she isn't capable of doing anything. Then all of a sudden a little spark appears and she smiles at me. Or she does things that she hasn't done for quite some time. This is really what motivates me. I say 'Dammit all, she can do it!' There are little things, like when I dress her in the morning, sometimes she is able to lift her foot so I can put her clothes on. And when she lifts her foot, I'm as happy as can be!

"Yes, deep down there is still very strong love on both sides. We still hold hands, you know."

Clearly, Tom is a first-rate caregiver—absolutely the right person for the job. Sometimes, however, someone giving care to an elder is not the right person for the job. Here is what Mindy Packer-Bloom, a social worker with the York regional government in Ontario, has to say on the topic.

"In my experience, caregiving is not always done voluntarily. It's often whoever gets chosen, or whoever is available. And it is not always a willing partnership between caregiver and care receiver. Often it is a daughter-in-law who is doing the job only because it's an obligation she has to her husband. Maybe the husband has sisters, but it's perceived as a son's responsibility in some cultures, so it falls on the daughter-in-law's shoulders. We see this a lot, and as a result of it there are a lot of resentful, burned-out caregivers."

As Tom Pope's story and Mindy Packer-Bloom's experiences demonstrate, filling the caregiver role is often a highly emotional experience and one requiring self-knowledge and wisdom. Consider this book to be a journey that will prepare you for the caregiving experience. The first step involves asking the critical question of whether you should be the primary caregiver. Further stages of the journey include adjusting family roles, helping care receivers remain healthy in later life and looking after someone who is confined to bed. In the final phase, the caregiver must rethink his or her role when the elder is admitted into permanent care.

In many cases, of course, the caregiver role falls automatically on the shoulders of a disabled care receiver's healthier partner. Most often, the caregiver is the woman; usually younger than her partner, she is likely to be in better health. You might think that, for such caregivers, the question of whether the role is an appropriate one never should arise. But this is not necessarily so. Consider, for instance, the hypothetical case of a man who becomes the caregiver for his wife, who has had a massive stroke. The husband has a history of wife abuse. While some caregiving duties will, of necessity, fall to him, he should consider sharing the role with someone else, perhaps a family member or a professional caregiver. Relieved of at least part of his burden, he will probably be far less likely to become abusive once more.

The purpose of this chapter, then, is to help you find out whether you are the right person to assume the caregiver role, and to examine your alternatives to shouldering the burden alone.

Things to Do Before Assuming the Caregiver Role

If you know any other informal (familial or friendly) caregivers, talk to them at length. They will be able to tell you what to expect in the role, what is enjoyable about it, and what may be disagreeable. If you feel you'll need help of some kind, ask them where they found help when they needed it. Also ask them if they would be willing to share with you the knowledge they gleaned from mistakes they may have made in the role.

Talk to members of your immediate family. If you assume the caregiver role, this will probably bring about changes in the living patterns of your partner and children, especially if the care receiver will come to live in your home. Even if you live in separate homes, you will have less time to be with family members. They deserve a chance to voice their opinions about this.

Don't let other family members force the caregiving role on you. Perhaps they are turning their backs on the situation, or finding all kinds of reasons why they are too busy to be caregivers, or telling you that you are the best suited for this kind of work. You and your immediate family should be the ones making the decision.

Don't act hastily. If, for instance, your father dies, don't take your mother into your home right away. She may not want to move. You and your immediate family need time to consider the implications of such an action.

Examine your own feelings and attitudes and those of the person needing care. Do you really want to be a caregiver to this person, or are you about to take on the role out of a sense of duty or guilt? If you are driven by duty or guilt, and if someone else is available whose motivation is better, you should perhaps encourage that person to become the caregiver. Does the person needing care want you to be the primary caregiver? Finding the right answers to questions such as these calls for some clear thinking and some good communication on the part of all those involved, with no pressure and with complete honesty.

Helping Elders Remain Independent

Remember one critical fact. A loss of independence, the ability to make choices about how to live one's life, automatically brings with it a loss of dignity. You would not enjoy this. Nor will your potential care receiver.

Most elders prefer to live separately from their adult children—not surprisingly, since this means they are truly independent. So if your parent or other elder is capable of living alone, don't even think of a move—especially if a move would mean the elder would have to leave a familiar and well-loved community and friends.

Even if your elder can't live alone without a considerable amount of help, you may decide not to move him or her into your home. Yes, you will have to assume the responsibility for running two households. But the elder will not suffer a great loss of independence, and your household will not experience the disruption the elder's presence might cause.

Just as they wish not to be dependent on adult children by living with them, many elders—usually younger ones—prefer to remain independent of family help and instead hire professional caregivers when they can afford to do so. By doing this, they are not placing a burden on their loved ones. And they prefer that professional people rather than family members give them care that involves intimacy so that neither party will be embarrassed. If any elders of yours opt for professional versus family caregiving, don't try to change their minds.

Lise, Carmelle and Serge: Caregivers for the Right Reasons

To decide whether you will become a caregiver for the right reasons, consider the three thumbnail sketches below, and try to estimate what your response would be to caregiving in each case.

Lise Nikolaisen's 60-year-old husband has multiple sclerosis. Lise, 50, has been his sole caregiver for about 15 years. "He is mine. He is the love of my life, my idol, and I don't want someone else looking after him," she says. She has to do just about everything for him, including shaving him and brushing his teeth. "It isn't a problem for me," she says. "I do this out of love and devotion to my husband."

She adds, "A caregiver should not forget her church if she is religious. It can be very helpful. And if you believe, which I do very much, that is where you will get your strength from."

Carmelle Harrison, 60, caregiver to her husband Patrick until his death at the age of 93, also cites her faith as a source of support. "There are all kinds of rewards in caregiving," she says. "I believe this is a call from God, and coping with it is a form of personal grace, a period of purification. My husband's illness taught me a lot, not something that will make me rich, but something that will make me a better person."

Indeed, Carmelle had much to cope with. Patrick was completely incapacitated by a combination of Alzheimers and Parkinsons. "He couldn't speak or move and had a hard time opening his eyes," she says. "But he loved to be loved, to have me hold his hand."

Serge Couturier, 37, has been his 68-year-old mother's caregiver since 1990. She has been helpless since she had a massive stroke; she cannot walk or speak, and Serge has to do almost everything for her. This is pretty well a full-time job, which Serge can do since he has gastric problems and is permanently off work and drawing down a disability pension. He is also single, so there are no demands on his time by a wife or children. His father, for whom he was also a caregiver, is no longer alive. He has five brothers and one sister; the latter occasionally comes to help him out. But, he says, "my mother prefers that I take care of her. She feels more comfortable and more protected with me."

Case workers have suggested to Serge that he lighten the burden he has shouldered by putting his mother in permanent care, which, they advise him, is where someone so massively disabled belongs. Serge disagrees. "My mother needs to stay here at home. She is relatively young, she is conscious. I love her a lot and she has always been very good to me. She is a perfect mother, and it is a priority in my life to take care of her."

Self-Tests #1 and #2: For Potential Caregivers and Care Receivers

If you have any doubts about whether you should be the primary or sole caregiver, we recommend that you and your care receiver each complete the following self-tests. You should both work through the tests without talking to anyone else about your answers, and you should not show each other your answers. Instead, when the worksheets are completed, you should submit them for analysis to an objective third person with expertise in relationships. This person will then help you reach a decision, and may also initiate discussions among the three of you to facilitate this process.

If you do not know such a person, ask your family physician's advice or seek counsel from a public health nurse or staff at the local family services association. To contact a public health nurse, refer to the municipal government section of the blue pages in your telephone directory; you'll find there a listing for "Health Services," "Health Care Services" or "Public Health Services." To reach the family services association, which may be called a family counseling centre or family life bureau, look in the Yellow Pages under "Social Service Organizations."

SELF-TEST #1

How do I feel about my care receiver?

- Have I ever felt exasperated, frustrated, resentful or angry because of this person's behavior or mindset?
- Have I ever been abused, physically or otherwise, by this person?
- Am I planning on becoming the primary caregiver out of a sense of duty or guilt?
- If the care receiver is my partner, have we always faced hardships in a unified way?
- As a partner, can I state that our relationship has always been and still is marked by love and loyalty?

How do I feel about the role?

- Have I any experience of giving care to an elderly person?
- Do I usually not enjoy being with older people?
- Do I mind being with someone who has some disability?
- Will I resent having to spend a lot of time with this person?

- Do I dislike touching other people? (This elder may need nursing care.)
- If this person develops cognitive or behavioral problems, will I cope well? (Problems could include forgetfulness, wandering, or delusions.)

How do I cope with stress?

- Am I a poor listener? For instance, if this person voices the same complaint six times, will I become angry?
- Do I mind waiting for others to finishing doing something, such as eating dinner or telling a story?
- Do I resort to using alcohol or other drugs to help me get through the day?

General

- Is this person asking me to become the primary caregiver?
- If so, why have I not offered my services?
- Has this person ever expressed hostile feelings towards me?
- Do I believe this person will accept my help willingly?
- Do I dread my own aging? (If so, I may find watching someone else age highly disturbing.)
- Do I spend much time feeling depressed and sorry for myself?
- Do ailing people annoy me, perhaps because they become the centre of attention?
- This person may become severely disabled and may die in my home and in my presence. Will this greatly upset me?
- Am I the person most suited to this caregiver role?

SELF-TEST #2

Now here's the self-test for the potential care receiver. If this person cannot write well or has vision problems, ask a third person to help out by writing down the answers and/or reading out the questions.

Thoughts and emotions

- Do I believe this person will be able to care for me properly?
- Can I accept help from this person happily?
- Am I in general willing to accept help from people?
- Will I feel myself to be a burden to this person?
- Will I be willing to live with this caregiver's ground rules regarding mealtimes, bedtimes and so on?
- If my would-be caregiver becomes stressed and easily angered at things I do or say, will I be able to accept this?
- Have I coerced this person into being my caregiver with a promise of financial generosity in the future?
- My condition may deteriorate to the point where this person has to bathe me and perform other intimate functions. Will I greatly mind this?
- If my answer to the last question was yes, would I prefer to be in the hands of professional caregivers?
- Would I generally feel safer and happier living in a retirement home?

The relationship

- Did this person offer to be my caregiver?
- If an offer was not made, do I know why not?
- Do I love and hold in high regard this person?

- Has my past relationship with this person been good?
- Is this the right person to be my primary caregiver?

CHAPTER TWO

Assessing the Level of Care Needed and Your Ability to Provide It

Torontonian Mary Allen-Armiento, 66, was her mother's caregiver for nine years until the latter's death in 1994. Her mother had Alzheimers and was also incontinent. Mary, a single parent, had to quit her job, one which she greatly enjoyed, in order to look after her mother. Consequently, she had to use the money she had put aside for her daughter's higher education to meet her and her mother's living expenses.

Her mother originally spent six years in a retirement home. But she began "misbehaving," in the words of the home's staff. They wanted her to socialize with other residents, but she preferred reading. They said to her, "Now we are going to have a bath." And she replied, "We are? Well, you have it first." They finally declared she was paranoid— at which point Mary took her out of the home.

Mary's mother first went to live with Mary's brother in Sudbury. But almost immediately he called her and said he couldn't cope with the caregiver role and was sending his mother south to her. "He didn't ask me," Mary recalls. "But I could see why. After all, my sister-in-law is not directly related to my mother. And Alzheimers behavior is hard to cope with."

Soon after she moved in with Mary, her mother began wandering at night. People in the apartment below told the landlord and he told Mary she and her mother would have to move out. She had no ready cash; her savings were all tied up in RRSPs. But friends rallied round and pitched in so that she was able to put a down payment on a townhouse. "Dante said, 'When you have a friend you have a treasure,'" she says happily. "Well, with friends like mine, I was surrounded by treasures."

She was so hard up, she recalls, that one Christmas she had just $2. "So I went out and bought a nice soup bone and made soup."

She has since paid back all but $1,000 of the money her friends lent her. She hopes to find work as a babysitter to pay off that last debt. However, she says, "I feel a little pain that my daughter is saddled with more than $20,000 of debt for her schooling."

Ideally, Mary Allen-Armiento should not have been her mother's caregiver. She had to give up a career she greatly enjoyed and she didn't have the financial wherewithal to allow them to live comfortably. But she feels good about the decision to look after her mother. "I did it for love," she says. "When my mother died, I had no guilt. Whether I did right or wrong, I did my best. I'm so glad I did it."

Just as Chapter One showed how potential caregivers can measure their psychological and emotional ability to fill the role, this chapter shows how they can measure their physical and material ability to give care.

As a potential primary caregiver, you should be concerned about three measures: temporal, financial, and physical. You will need sufficient spare time and money to do a good job of caregiving. Physical issues to be considered include having adequate house room if the would-be care receiver will be moving in with you, and having the health, stamina and strength should you need to help someone who may be large and heavy.

How Much Care Is Needed?

First you must find out how much care this person actually needs. Much of this you can determine from your own observations. For instance, if this person is able to bathe, dress, use the toilet and prepare and eat food, the caregiving role will not be too onerous. Similarly, if this person is able to do house and yard work, go shopping, use public transit or taxis and handle personal finances, the amount of caregiving required will be minimal.

If you need specialized help to find out how much care this person actually needs, Dr. Cyril Gryfe, an internist geriatrician on the staff of North York General Hospital, suggests a formal assessment should be made by a geriatric psychiatrist or an internist geriatrician.

You might also have the assessment done by a geriatric assessment unit, or GAU. GAUs work out of hospitals or health care centres. The individuals comprising a GAU may include any or all of the following: physician, therapist, gerontological nurse, social worker, pharmacist and dietitian. To contact a GAU, ask your family physician, another health care worker or a social worker for a reference. Do not contact a GAU directly.

Two final thoughts on caregiving. The amount of care a person needs will most likely increase over time, and may become more complicated. And you should be prepared for the fact that, since human longevity has increased greatly, you may be making a long-term commitment.

The Need for Time

Margaret McArthur, a community health nurse in York Region, tells of two sisters who are quickly running out of time. Their mother is normally their father's caregiver, but she had to go into hospital for an extensive period. Both daughters have jobs, so the ideal course of action would have been to bring in professional caregivers. "But one daughter keeps saying, 'Well you know, they are very private people and they won't have anyone else come in.' Older people are often afraid someone is going to steal something," McArthur says. So the daughters have been taking vacation days, one taking three days one week and the other two, and vice versa the following week. "They say, 'We can do it for a little while,'" McArthur says. "Well they have been doing it for almost four months and their holidays are running out."

The sisters, of course, are counting on their mother's recovery. And maybe they are right. But they would still have done better to call in professional help because looking after their father was clearly a time-consuming job. Their solution was not a realistic one.

When you estimate how much time will be needed to adequately perform the caregiver role, you must be highly realistic. For instance, if you have already determined that the amount of caregiving required will be minimal, you can probably assume caregiving will not take up much time, while if you realize a lot of care will be necessary, you can probably assume the role will be onerous.

Now here's a self-test to help you measure your temporal ability to give care. As with all self-tests, don't rush your answers. Give careful consideration to each question first.

SELF-TEST #3

- Have I considered all the ways in which this person will need my help?
- Do I have a realistic estimate of the amount of time I will spend in caregiving?
- How many hours a day do I currently spend maintaining my home and looking after my immediate family?
- Would becoming a caregiver to this person mean he or she would move into my home? Would this increase the time spent doing housework?
- If this person will not move into my home, how much time will be spent commuting between homes?
- Would it be feasible to telephone daily and so limit visiting to two or three times a week?
- Will I be able to call on others, such as relatives, neighbors or friends, to help out in various ways (visiting, going out to a restaurant or a movie or acting as chauffeur)?
- If I am a caregiver to others—my children perhaps—will being a caregiver to this person have a negative affect on my other care receivers?
- If I am employed, will being a caregiver mean I will have to work only part time or perhaps not at all?
- If I have to work part time or not at all, will this mean the end of a career?
- If it will indeed mean the end of a career, will I resent this deeply?
- Will assuming the caregiving role deprive me of important social activity?

The Financial Burden of Caregiving

Carol Thompson, 54, of Campbell River, B.C., has been her husband John's caregiver for more than six years. He is 53 and suffers from bipolar affective disorder (BAD), or manic depression as it used to be known. "He didn't have much of a life before, but now that he has been diagnosed and is on medication, he has a normal life for long periods," she says.

Because of the demands of her role as caregiver, the only paid work she can do is babysitting. "Where else am I going to get a job that I can take three weeks to a month off when he is not well, so I can stay home and look after him?" she says. "Where else can I get a job where I can take him with me?"

Asked whether she has run into problems she never anticipated, she answers with one word: "Money." She explains that when someone who has BAD is in a manic phase he or she may spend money like water. "He would take what money he had in his pocket and go to a thrift store in the middle of summer and buy up all the wool tuques, rather than save the money for food.

"At one point he went out and bought six boats, ranging from an eight-foot car topper to a 26-foot pleasure craft. And he was writing cheques for all kinds of things. He put us deeply in debt. I have been trying to unbury us ever since."

This upset her, she says, "But I still love him. Because when he is well, he is a terrific person—very kind, compassionate, and loving."

You are not likely to have a financial problem of the magnitude of Carol's. But if becoming the primary caregiver will mean becoming the source of financial support, do plenty of calculating to determine whether you will have sufficient funds. And bear in mind that even if caregiving would not cost you dearly right now, later it might cost a great deal more.

If you have to partially or wholly support this person, the two of you should discuss this. Many people have difficulty talking about money matters, but it's important to raise this issue.

If paid services will be necessary, let the recipient pay for them if possible. Being independent and autonomous is important. If you will have to pay for them, be aware that this financial obligation may enhance the stresses you will experience as a caregiver.

Now here's another self-test, this time to help you measure your financial ability to give care.

SELF-TEST #4

- Is this person financially independent, with sufficient pension benefits, insurance, and other assets, to cope with any emergency situations?

- If she or he is housebound, will this person give me power of attorney so that I can withdraw money to make any necessary purchases?

- Has some other family member already been given power of attorney? If so, will this person revoke it and give me, as primary caregiver, power of attorney?

- Or, if someone else has power of attorney, will that person provide me with the funds I will need to cover the cost of caregiving? (If your answer here is "Yes," get that person to give you a written undertaking. People can—and do—change their minds.)

- Do I have sufficient assets to be able to assume the costs of caregiving without touching my retirement savings and hence imperiling my own old age?

- Will I be financially dependent on this person for both of our needs?

- If my answer to that last question is "Yes," how will I manage financially when this person goes into permanent care or dies?

- Will any other family members be willing to contribute funds to help support this person and/or me?

- If I have become accustomed to earning an income as a reward for my services, will I be able to accept the role of unpaid caregiver if this will indeed be the case?

- Do I expect or want a monetary reward for becoming a caregiver to this person?

- If my answer here is "Yes," have we discussed this? If so, what was the outcome? (If the answer was an agreement to give you money, get this in writing, too.)

- If giving care means I will have to give up my job, will this place a financial burden on my partner or other family members?

- Do I realize that not all support services available in the community are free and that I may need funds to hire help?

- Have I sufficient funds to cover future costs for supplies and support services should those costs rise and/or should this person's condition worsen?

- Have I taken account of any costs that may be incurred in modifying the home and providing assistive aids?

- If I find I am not suited to caregiving, could I afford to remunerate someone else for being the caregiver?

The Physical Aspects of Caregiving

A Toronto-area woman is the primary caregiver to her 89-year-old mother, who is in relatively good health, given her age. The mother does things around the house, such as setting the table before meals and helping her daughter clear it off afterwards. They also go out some afternoons to a doughnut shop for coffee.

One great benefit that being her mother's caregiver brought to this woman—and indeed to her entire family, for she has a husband and young children—was a move to a larger house. " I wanted a bungalow," the caregiver says, "but it is impossible to find one in this area. So we had to take a two-storey one. I've wanted to put a chairlift in because she has trouble walking, but she keeps saying, 'I can make those stairs!'

"She has the master bedroom, which has an adjacent bathroom, so she is self-contained up there."

If becoming a caregiver would mean having an elder come to live in your house, realize that changes may not be for the better, as they were for this family.

When considering whether you have sufficient health, stamina and perhaps strength, to be a good and effective caregiver, bear in mind that more demands may be made on you in later years when your own health and stamina may have deteriorated. But also bear in mind that you can obtain devices to help you lift or move someone. You'll learn about some of these in Chapter Ten.

Now here's another self-test, this time one to help you measure your physical ability to give care.

SELF-TEST #5

- If this person will live in my home, is the home safe for someone who is or may become frail and/or confused? If not, can I make the necessary modifications—grab bars, widened doorways and a ramp in place of steps to accommodate a wheelchair or a chairlift for someone who can't climb stairs, for instance?

- Will any family members have to share a room in order to free up a room for this person?

- If this person moves in, will there be enough private space for everyone?

- Am I physically strong enough that I will be able to help this person bodily, perhaps lifting him or her into and out of a bath?

- Am I in good enough mental and physical health to be able to fill the demanding role of caregiver possibly for many years without becoming exhausted or burned out?

- Do I have any experience of first aid procedures such as disinfecting and dressing sores, scratches and ulcers, bandaging a sprained ankle or wrist or cutting ingrown toenails?

- If I don't have any such experience, am I willing to take a first aid course?

- Are all of us in the family prepared in every way to give shelter, companionship and help to this person—and to give added help if and when disabilities cause it to be needed?

CHAPTER THREE

Family and Friends' Roles and Relationships

"I tell people considering bringing a parent into their home, 'You'd better think about this in advance.' It's just different interests and different lifestyles put together. My mother was a quiet person. She was happy doing her own thing. But we also had noisy teenagers in the house doing *their* thing. As the person in the middle, I was trying to look after everybody's welfare, and it became a tussle. Your sons and your husband want to go canoeing this weekend, but this would leave your mother on her own. She doesn't like being on her own, so what do you do? It's a trivial thing. But, as a friend of mine once said, 'When you have them live with you, they trivialize you to death.' She was right; it's the trivial things that cause the ongoing stress. And then you feel guilty about getting upset because it's trivial."

Pat Gray knows well what she is talking about: she has been a caregiver three times over—to her own mother, whom she brought over from England to live with her in Winnipeg after the death of her father, and to her husband John's parents, who lived in Victoria. And she is absolutely right. A number of the people with expertise who were interviewed to gather material for this book stressed that caregivers must set routines for dealing with relatively minor affairs well in advance, since some older people become quite upset by even small changes of plan.

When someone is about to become a care receiver, the effect is rather like taking a magnifying glass to a whole web of relationships—between caregiver and care receiver, between caregiver and other family members, and within individual families. Unless dealt with promptly and effectively, small irritants can grow to become large stumbling blocks. In this chapter, we'll examine some of those relationships and how best they may be handled.

Mary Allen-Armiento is a member of a Toronto-area support group for primary caregivers. Her own experiences, coupled with information gleaned from other members of the group, have given her more insights into caregiving than many laypeople possess. "It's important the family realizes what it may be getting into," Mary says. "Families should sit down and talk it through in advance. You have to think about things you may have to give up. Because if you're going to resent those losses, that's when the abuse may come."

If you are a daughter considering caring for your mother, you should be aware that daughters often become more stressed than sons when they become maternal caregivers, probably because mother–daughter relationships are usually complex and can be charged with conflicting emotions.

As well, if you are contemplating becoming a caregiver to a parent because you believe this action will earn you the love you never received from her or him, think again. Roles may change, but attitudes usually don't.

Also consider the fact that if you become a primary caregiver, your partner—and your children at home if you have any—may become highly jealous of the care receiver, since you are now giving this person the time and attention you formerly gave your family. Often, these emotions don't surface at the outset, but take the form of a slow burn.

Mary recalls a case of such jealousy. A woman took her mother out of a nursing home and began to care for her in her own home. The mother could not climb stairs, so she slept on the ground floor. She had Alzheimers, so the daughter could not leave her alone. This meant that she too had to sleep downstairs. This made her husband irate. "So there was the threat of breaking up a marriage," Mary says. "And you ask yourself, 'Who comes first? What do I do?' This was a torn woman."

The marriage survived, but the husband had to learn to calm down.

This anecdote leads to another important point. If you are contemplating caregiving in your own home, you should be aware that, not surprisingly, the presence of a mentally impaired elder in a home is often more damaging to family relationships than the presence of a physically impaired person.

Before becoming a caregiver, seek counsel so that you will understand in advance how your life and your relationships with others may change. Professional counsel is available from staff at your local family service association (go back to Chapter One if you don't recall how to locate an association near you), or a social worker, or members of a geriatric assessment unit. Or you might attend several meetings of a local caregivers' support group and talk to members about their experiences. (Chapter Fourteen contains information on how to locate a support group.) Or, if the potential care receiver suffers from a specific chronic condition, talk to staff at the organization that helps people with that condition. For instance, if this person has diabetes, seek counsel from your local branch of the Canadian Diabetes Association.

As well, try to become knowledgeable about facets of caregiving. For instance, be on the lookout for seminars or information meetings about caregiver–care receiver relationships. Read books on the subject, watch television or listen to radio programs on the topic. You need to know all you can about the possible relationship between elders and their adult children, about the effects on the children of proximity to the elder, and about the process of aging.

Ground Rules for Live-in Caregiving

Barbara Burns is a social worker who also teaches and lectures on caregiving at Carleton University and elsewhere in Ottawa. She has herself been a caregiver, so she has a dual insight into the role and what it entails. "When all generations agree that combining households would be a positive step, some formal ground rules must be established in advance and agreed to by all," she counsels. "Experience has shown that if issues of private time, of division of household responsibilities and finances, of holiday schedules, and of socializing are not settled, they become the potential battlefields of the future."

She also recommends that decisions regarding practical matters be made in advance. Should the incoming elder have her or his own telephone line, for instance? Should the entire household sit down to meals together? How might weekend activities require rescheduling once the household expands?

If all this advance consideration and planning still leaves you not completely sure whether taking this elder into your home would be a good and rewarding experience, another course of action is possible. Have a trial run of, say, three months. If you take this course, realize in advance there will be some hurt feelings if things don't work out. So make sure all those involved, and especially the elder, understand that this is indeed a trial run and that a more permanent stay will not be contemplated unless all those involved agree to it.

If you are considering caregiving in your home to a parent, your mother perhaps, because her partner has just died, don't move her in right away, either on a trial basis or permanently. Bereavement counselors emphasize that, if at all possible, no move should be made until one to two years have elapsed following the death of a spouse.

But what if your mother says she wants to move in now? Talk to her, find out why she wants to do this. She is probably feeling lonely, insecure, frightened and in need of attention.

So far as insecurity and fear are concerned, point out that there are all kinds of security devices on the market, among them alarm systems and emergency call devices. Local police forces will often do security checks of homes and make recommendations. And, Burns adds, "a dog might also be considered to act as a deterrent with the added benefits of companionship and a stimulus for exercise."

So far as loneliness is concerned, occupying her time with useful work will be a great help. Encourage her to do volunteer work. Newspapers often carry lists of services needing volunteers. Or call a local central volunteer bureau to find out what opportunities there are.

And so far as needing attention is concerned, visit her frequently in her own home if you can, and encourage other family members to do so as well. If she has friends who don't know she has been widowed, let them know and ask them if they will visit too—or, if they live at a distance, write to her.

Good and Bad Family Relationships

Wayne Sigen, a 50-year-old accountant living in Scarborough, Ontario, has been a caregiver to both his grandparents and his parents. "I and my wife and my brother and his wife are all helping out," he says. "It's just a matter of spreading the work around."

In a similar vein, Elizabeth Shantz, a supervisor in the Durham Region health department, teams up with her brother to look after the affairs of their two elderly parents. "My brother and I have joint power of attorney," she says. "Until recently my father managed his finances. I am managing them now, but I always tell my brother what I am doing and consult with him.

"There was a time when my mother was getting really tired, and my dad needed to go into respite care to give her a break. Well, he wasn't buying into that, so we staged a family conference one Friday night—my brother, father, mother and me. I moderated over it, we all said our piece and we worked through the problem."

There are several reasons for taking a team approach to caregiving.

First, if functions are shared out fairly evenly, no one caregiver will bear a really heavy load.

Second, if you were the sole caregiver and you had an accident, who would look after your care receiver? If you have taken a team approach, there will always be a backup in the case of an emergency.

Third, the care receiver may well enjoy interacting with two or more people instead of being in regular contact with only one.

Finally, different people have different skills. Maybe one member of the team is good at managing money, while another is good at giving hands-on care.

One team approach that is not recommended is rotation. In other words, if an elder has three adult children, all living in their own homes, the elder spends four months of each year in each household. At any age, few people would want to live such a nomadic life, and the older people are, the more resistant they generally become to change.

If you have not taken the team approach, once you have assumed the role of caregiver you're quite likely to find that siblings and other relatives leave you to do the job and don't offer to help. As you already know, there is a down side to being a sole caregiver, so if they don't offer to help, you should ask them to do so.

Barbara Burns has a telling anecdote about a caregiver who didn't ask for help. Her relatives came to visit, but made no offer of help. "I finally asked her, 'Did you ask them?' and her reply was an outburst: 'They should be able to see!' Well, in this case it was in relation to money, and money is really hard to see, you know. If you are short of money, it's not always apparent.

"So I said, 'Maybe if you asked them . . .' and she said, 'Oh, I couldn't do that.' So I suggested she put it in writing in a letter. That she *was* able to do. She described the situation, and they came across with some help."

You may have to be quite insistent when you ask for assistance because you may receive all kinds of excuses as to why people can't help. If you ask someone to look after your care receiver over the weekend because you'd like to rest up or have activities you want to pursue, you'll probably be told, "No, I can't, I'm afraid. I have all kinds of things to do this weekend."

Perhaps one of the most ridiculous excuses for not coming to help was told to Carmelle Harrison, the former caregiver and caregiver activist. A woman caregiver who badly needed to take a break wrote to her brothers and sisters, who lived in another province, asking for short-term help. "They wrote back that they wanted to remember their mother the way she was," Carmelle says. "Lovely, eh?"

If you do not get help and support from others, you will likely suffer. If your spouse, siblings and children refuse to become involved in caregiving, you may become increasingly isolated from other family members because you simply do not have time for them. And you may be severely stressed. Even if the caregiver burden is not a heavy one, carrying it alone will almost certainly be stressful.

Talking Things Out

People who agree to help should be allowed to have some choice as to the form of help they'll give. Maybe, for instance, you have a neighbor who's a keen gardener and could help you out from time to time with yard work. Maybe a sister is a great cook and might come over once or twice a week and make dinner for the whole family.

Make sure that some of the help you are given also gives you time out. Perhaps your mother goes to a brother's house on Sunday for lunch and stays until late afternoon. Perhaps she goes to stay with your sister and her husband for a week or two in late spring so that you and your partner can take a short vacation. Maybe a nephew takes your mother out for drives in the country when the weather is good.

Even relatively young children can help out by being with your care receiver while you attend to other matters. A boy who has recently learned to read will enjoy showing off his abilities to a grandparent. Boys and girls are also likely to enjoy playing board and card games with their grandparents.

If caregiving will be a family endeavor—whether this means a team comprised of a primary caregiver, her or his siblings, and the care receiver's grandchildren, or simply one primary and one secondary caregiver—open and frank communication is essential if the endeavor is to succeed.

This communication begins before caregiving itself does. All those involved should meet to discuss how the various responsibilities would best be shared. If the team is comprised of four people or more, you might consider asking each person to arrive with a "wish list" of activities she or he would be willing to undertake. Before decisions are taken, make clear to everyone that this will in effect be a trial run. If it later seems that a better division of responsibilities exists, appropriate changes will be made.

A potential care receiver who is not cognitively impaired should take part in the discussion and make some decisions, for instance, expressing a desire that a particular sibling be put in charge of financial matters. If the elder is present, however, you must all take care how you phrase your remarks so that you don't voice sentiments that make caregiving sound like an unwelcome chore.

If the elder is not to be present, at least let him or her know that you are meeting to discuss how to share out responsibilities. In so doing you are not going behind this person's back. You are also giving him or her a chance to express wishes or caveats.

When discussing future arrangements, you might say to the elder, "One of the things we want to be really careful of is that we don't tread on your toes." This gets the message across that you are going to value and honor this person's independence and autonomy, and also subtly gets across your expectation of reciprocal respect.

Establishing timetables should also be done at the outset. If the new member of the household will have a separate apartment with a kitchen, for instance, everyone, including the elder, should agree on what days and at what times the elder should join the rest of the family for meals. If the timetables set later prove unworkable, meet again so that you can all approve changes.

Whether an elder is living alone or with a primary caregiver, regular meetings to make sure that everything is working out well are not necessary. A caregiving team need meet only when conditions change, or when one member of the team calls for a meeting for a justifiable reason.

If, for whatever reason, team members cannot agree upon a decision and meetings deteriorate into arguments, consider calling in a third person to help you reach a decision that all can accept. A social worker or public health nurse accustomed to dealing with older people and caregivers might be the chosen mediator. So might a member of the clergy.

Communicating well also means planning ahead for probable critical events well before they happen. For instance, you might want a caregiver group to discuss what should be done if your mother, a widow who now lives alone, becomes unable to care for herself on a day-to-day basis. Ideally all members of the family should meet to discuss such eventualities, but if some live at a distance, they should participate fully in all discussions and decisions either by telephone or in writing.

Care Receiver Behaviors

Pat Gray has a telling ancedote about her mother. "She felt, I think, that she had to earn her stay here, so she was always very helpful with the housework. We divvied it up that I cooked meals and she did the dishes afterwards. But she felt a bit like she was a guest in the house, and this went on until a funny and picky episode."

It happened one evening when her mother yanked her headphone cord out of the TV somewhat roughly. John, Pat's husband, told her sharply not to do that, and she went off in a huff to her room. Pat told John he had upset her mother. "So he went to her room and said, 'Mum, I'm sorry I snapped at you, but that happens in families.' The whole atmosphere changed from that day on because he'd said, 'It happens in families.' She realized she had been accepted into the family."

Pat's mother may have had another motive in helping with the housework. Nobody likes to feel put out to pasture, no longer part of the world of the living. Unless they are very infirm, care receivers want responsibilities, a sense that they are participants in life, not mere spectators. As a caregiver, you may sometimes feel you have too many responsibilities. Consider passing some of them along; your care receiver may gladly accept them—and, in so doing, feel part of the family.

If your care receiver is living with you or is about to come to live with you, one responsibility might be financial. For instance, your mother might say, "You take me many places in the car—to the bank, to the doctor, for outings on the weekend, shopping and so on.

I'd like to pay half your gas bill." Accept with a smile. Now your mother feels part of the family because she is contributing something. She has dignity because she is not totally dependent on someone else to provide for her.

Barbara Burns feels very strongly about this. "The big thing about growing old is that people feel useless," she says. "They lose all their roles. If you can give a role back to them in any way, it helps them greatly and it helps you too in the long run. It could be something as small as 'Please hold the wool for me while I wind it.'"

You may have to be a little inventive in providing roles for your care receiver. Maybe an elder wants to do the dishes—despite the fact that you have a dishwasher —but you're concerned that some of your precious crockery or glassware may fall from enfeebled hands and break. Stack the dishes and glasses in the dishwasher and leave pots, pans and cutlery for your care receiver to do.

A caregiver living in Scarborough, Ontario, recalls that after her mother came to live with her and her family, her mother said she just couldn't cope with having noisy teenagers coming in and out all the time.

The caregiver, who was working part-time, realized there was no easy solution to her mother's complaints. Her mother was 89 and deserving of consideration, and she was unable to quiet her teenaged children. Her solution, obviously not an ideal one, was to give up her part-time job so that she could pack the kids away when her mother wanted to come down from her room.

Sometimes there are no easy answers when trying to cope with care receiver behaviors that stress the caregiver. But if the caregiver understands the motive behind the behaviors, they become easier to bear.

For instance, a care receiver may continually call for the caregiver to "Please come here and tuck the rug under my knees," or "I'm cold —bring me a cardigan" or "I don't like this program—please change the TV station." Recognize that the problem quite likely is not a slipped rug, coldness or a dislike of a TV program. Quite simply, this person probably wants company. And if you are the caregiver in question, you clearly can't get any work done if you grant every request. You could try pointing this out to the elder, discussing what might be a reasonable compromise. Or, if you have children, one solution might be to ask the children to spend time with their grandparent when they are not in school. Or you might settle your care receiver in the room where you do much of your work—in front of a television set in the kitchen while you are cooking or doing dishes, perhaps.

A care receiver who once had great skills at certain tasks may have to turn over those tasks to a caregiver. Perhaps your mother was a terrific cook, but now you must do the cooking. She may rail against your efforts, saying they are far inferior to the dishes she once made. You will find these comments easier to bear if you realize that at least part of her rage is not at you but at the fact that she can no longer cook and has had to hand over control to you.

In a like vein, if a care receiver has a stroke and subsequently starts lashing out verbally—and perhaps even physically—at a care receiver, at least part of the anger is over the stroke and the disabilities it has caused. In this case, you should try saying something like "It must be terrible not to be able to express yourself clearly. Is there some way I can help you? What about paper and pencil?"

In short, you must realize that it is the disease and not the person that is talking. And keep on reminding yourself of this fact, since acceptance may take a long time—years even.

A care receiver may refuse to do what you ask or criticize your efforts in several areas. This person is probably trying to exercise a measure of control and, in the case of refusals, to remain independent. Elders feel loss of control and independence keenly. Try to understand this. Be patient. Give this person a measure of control wherever possible. And don't take criticism too seriously.

You may find that an elder suddenly starts to talk constantly about minor complaints and becomes totally preoccupied with her or his state of health. This person has not necessarily become self-centred or ailing overnight. Probably she or he is missing elements of life that were once enjoyed—choosing books at the library and chatting with the librarians, perhaps, or going shopping. Something must replace these lost activities, and what more natural than this person's own body, the nearest thing at hand? If you can recognize this, you are more likely not to become annoyed when your care receiver harps continually on minor ailments.

Sometimes an elder who has developed some physical disability—great weight gain or loss, perhaps, or loss of a limb or a breast—may reject a partner's advances and efforts to help because the partner will see the disability. If you are the caregiver in a case like this, and if you are not uncomfortable with the disability, try to alleviate this person's fear and discomfort and give him or her a hug. If indeed you are uncomfortable, you need the help of a secondary caregiver if this elder needs assistance with such activities as bathing.

If you are caring both for an elder and for adolescent children in your home, you may find the elder has an annoying tendency to get involved in altercations you have with your children. Perhaps you are not happy with some of the friendships your son has struck up and are telling him so. If your father starts interrupting and voicing his opinion, try not to be annoyed. Your father is simply trying to exert some control over a situation. Tell him you greatly value his opinion on the subject, but in the short run you'd like to talk to your son by himself. Maybe he could leave you two alone now, then later you and he can have a good conversation on the subject and reach some long-term solutions.

Sibling Relationships

Relationships between siblings living at a distance from each other are particularly susceptible to stresses. Perhaps a brother lives at a distance from his sister, who is the primary caregiver to their mother. The brother arrives for a visit, harshly criticizes his sister's caregiving, showers his mother with attention and gifts, then retreats to his safe distance on the other side of the country.

Possibly the brother has always been the uninvolved child in the family. If this is the case, he is not going to change. But what if he was formerly an involved, caring child?

"When many of us experience an abrupt change in our lives — death, illness, some other tragedy—our instinctive response is to deny it," Barbara Burns explains. "After all, denial protects us. As the mother may deny deafness and decreased vision, so the son may deny his mother's changed condition. When one cannot be closely involved, it is sometimes less stressful to the psyche to deny that the parent is aging. Denial protects one from guilt.

"This defence may be reinforced by the mother, who avoids describing details of her health because she 'does not want to worry him.'"

As well, the primary caregiver, seeing the elder on a daily basis, probably does not notice minor changes, while the one living at a distance, who has not seen the elder for a year or more, may exclaim, "My God, why didn't you tell me how much worse she has become?"

The solution? Keep distant siblings informed of any changes on an ongoing basis, either by telephone or by writing.

Here's another common situation. You are a woman giving care to your father who until now has made all the decisions regarding the management of his finances and the day-to-day running of the household. Now he can no longer make such decisions, so the role of decision maker has become yours.

But you are wildly unsure of your ability to make the right decisions. Your instinct is to call on someone else, an older sister perhaps, to make the decisions instead. Try not to do this. Your sister probably doesn't want to have two people, you and your father, depending on her decisions. And you are probably better at making decisions than you realize. So start out with a compromise. Make a decision and, before implementing it, ask your sister, "Is this the right thing to do?" When you have been through this process several times and she has agreed with your decision on every occasion, you'll feel reassured and able to strike out on your own.

Here's an action one unselfish sibling can perform to benefit another. Say your sister is the sole caregiver to your parents, who are still living in their own home. She is in their home for extended periods every day. As well as owning their mortgage-free home, your parents have considerable means. When they die, your caregiving sister really deserves a larger share of the estate than do you or other siblings who have not been secondary caregivers. Someone should point this out to your parents so that they can give the matter due consideration and, if they agree, make her the prime beneficiary in their wills.

Former caregiver and caregiver activist Carmelle Harrison says, "Primary caregivers are often accused of elder abuse. The truth is caregivers are often abused by other members of the family. I know this because so many of us have lived it."

More often than not, this abuse is verbal, and more often than not, it is heaped on the primary caregiver by siblings who do not want any part of caregiving. You might hear comments such as, "You're a woman, the only daughter. That's what women are good for—caregiving." Or "You always were their favorite child so get in there and start caregiving." Or "Mom and Dad always gave you everything you wanted, so now it's your turn to put out."

If you are the butt of such comments, try not to be upset and counter them with the good reasons for having secondary caregivers, as discussed earlier in this chapter.

Secondary caregivers and other siblings may mistrust the primary caregiver, suspecting that she is mismanaging the care receiver's finances, perhaps taking money unbeknownst to her care receiver. The caregiver who is the money manager should keep a careful record of all financial transactions, both in and out, so that she can open the book to the mistrustful ones to prove that she is not guilty of any wrongdoing.

As well, all caregivers should keep records of the time they spend giving care. These will prove useful if family members or friends accuse them of not doing enough. And if caregivers relinquish the role, both these records and financial ones will provide useful information for their successors.

Sometimes two sibling caregivers may be in conflict. For instance, perhaps the elder has diabetes and the primary caregiver carefully monitors this person's diet and intake of sugar. One evening, when the primary caregiver is not in the room, the elder says to the sibling, "It won't hurt if I have that chocolate bar, will it?" And the sibling, not knowing that her mother has already consumed her daily allowance of sucrose, replies, "It won't hurt you, Mom, so long as you don't forget to take your diabetes medication."

When she learns about this episode, how should the primary caregiver respond to the situation? Well, her sibling has clearly acted out of ignorance, so, instead of becoming angry at the bad advice, she should quietly tell her sibling why eating a candy bar is harmful to someone with diabetes.

Seeing Elderly Parents As They Are

Understand that when you become a caregiver to a parent or parents, your way of looking at them and their emotions may have to change. Barbara Burns comments on this important point.

"The adult child who recognizes that denial, stubbornness, selective attention, complaining, and other behaviors are defensive responses to change and losses, learns not to react to the behaviors but to the reasons behind them. And the child who learns to see his or her parents as human beings—warts and all—with needs can then meet those needs.

"However, the adult child who still fearfully perceives his parents as all-powerful human beings who must be obeyed remains caught in a time warp, unable either to say 'No' to unwarranted requests or to accept the feelings and behaviors attached to aging."

Caregiving From a Distance

If you live some distance from your parents or other elders and they refuse to move closer to you, probably your most important task is to enlist the help of any of your elders' friends and neighbors who are willing to be your eyes and ears in your absence, and who agree to contact you immediately should there be any sign of trouble or of change requiring your attention and perhaps, for a short time, your presence. Also ensure that a trusted neighbor has a key to your parents' house so that, if one day no one stirs, the drapes remain closed and the mail remains uncollected, the neighbor can get in to check out the situation.

You should also obtain a telephone directory for the area in which the elders live. If a friend has called and told you outside help of some kind now seems to be needed, you can make some preliminary calls to determine what kind of help is available in the community.

If you arrange for services of any kind to be brought to the house, get to know some of the people who will be providing them, give them your telephone number and ask them to notify you right away if they see any changes requiring your attention.

If you have several siblings, take it in turn to call your parents on a regular basis. You should also all write regularly, enclosing any photos that may be of interest to the elders. Elders will also be interested in videotapes and audiotapes of family activities.

And, remembering the good relationships that often exist between elders and their grandchildren, encourage the grandchildren to write. They might also enclose photographs or perhaps drawings they have made.

CHAPTER FOUR

Understand What You Are In For

Carol Thompson, caregiver to her manic-depressive husband, John, has sound advice for anyone who has decided to be a primary caregiver.

"Make sure you know what it is you are getting into," she says. If your care receiver has a disability, "make sure you get all the literature on it and learn all there is to learn about the illness. For instance, I belong to the Canadian Mental Health Association."

Many caregivers have little idea what they have taken on, Carol says. Ironically, she was such a one. No one in John's family warned her, because no one knew what his problem was. "They always knew he was a little different. They thought he was a little eccentric. Well, he is a little more than eccentric!

"He was in one of his good periods when I met him and married him. For the first year, I had no idea. I thought he was a very compulsive person, very spontaneous. Then he started having these episodes." And that was when, at her insistence, he sought professional help, and was properly diagnosed and put on medication.

In this chapter, we'll look both at some of the effects of caregiving you may experience, and some of the changes your care receiver may experience as he or she ages. Let's start with the effects the role may have on you.

Negative Experiences Caregivers Undergo

As a primary caregiver, you have a 50% chance of experiencing some unpleasant effects of caregiving. And if you are a daughter who is a primary caregiver, you have a 75% chance of experiencing poor physical and emotional health, both produced by the stresses inherent in the job. You are also likely to experience loss of privacy and socialization, and to resent the caregiver role.

Among other negative symptoms caregivers report: anxiety, depression (which is especially common among those caring for people with Alzheimers and other forms of dementia), sleeplessness, irritability, emotional exhaustion, frustration, and guilt. Physical problems often cited include stress-induced ulcers and back problems caused by lifting and moving heavy elders.

Don't assume that because you have raised children you're prepared to care for an elder. Two factors make giving care to an elder more demanding than caring for a child. One, you have no idea how long you will have to fill the caregiver role, so you cannot plan for the future. Two, a child becomes more independent almost by the day, while caring for an elder is likely to become increasingly challenging as age takes its toll.

Former caregiver Carmelle Harrison says, "After a while, most of your friends drop you because they don't know how to help you. A lot of the married couples you had as friends will have faded into the background. Even the people in your own profession drop you. My husband was in mining, but we never heard from his business friends. It's sad."

As well, she adds, caregivers looking after someone with physical disabilities may find that strangers disapprove of them appearing in public, which produces a sense of isolation. On one occasion, a friend invited her and her husband out for a meal in a restaurant. Her husband was in a wheelchair. His hands were tremoring so badly—he had Parkinsons—that he could not feed himself. So she cut his food up for him and fed it to him in a spoon. "And a woman a couple of tables over kept glaring at me."

Another caregiver also experiences loneliness because her elderly mother is living with her. "I have felt trapped sometimes," she says, "because for six years I have almost never been able to say I am going out to meet friends for lunch. I have done it but I felt guilty all the time because I knew she was at home and couldn't get out."

As our lifespans increase, so may a caregiver's caring years. One survey showed that 38% of its respondents had been caregivers for between five and 10 years, while fully 13% had been caregivers for more than 10 years.

Increased lifespans have also produced arrangements whereby elders, some of them themselves not in good health, give care to older elders. Reported cases include a primary caregiver who had had a heart attack and another with the first symptoms of Alzheimers.

Many caregivers have great difficulty finding time to do any of the things they like to do, or simply to rest up for a while. If they do not manage to find the time, they will almost certainly experience considerable emotional stress.

One retired social worker in Montreal, who has been a caregiver, emphasizes the importance of time off. "Always try to find time for you—always," she says. "Sometimes the family ties are strong, and you feel guilty because you are not doing your best. But this is a guilt that kills. You must sometimes put the focus on yourself. Try to find time to do things you like doing."

Consequences of the Aging Process

All the changes described below are normal changes that may occur as a person ages. None of them should give you cause for alarm, unless they occur in extreme form. For instance, skin dryness is normal, and can be countered by using a good moisturizer or even baby oil. Psoriasis, which resembles a severe and widespread case of dry skin, should be treated by a physician.

As a caregiver, you should read this and the following pages carefully, for two reasons. One, if you are not prepared for the changes your care receiver will experience as he or she ages, you may be emotionally stressed, even shocked, when these changes occur. And two, as noted above, you need to be able to distinguish between normal conditions and ones that call for specialized attention.

Changes in Hair, Facial and Neck Skin and Complexion

Graying and thinning of hair is common in many people. Loss of hair, both on the head and the body, may be gradual.

New, coarse, short hairs may start growing—in men in the nose, ears and eyebrows, in women on the chin. Many women over 70 grow hair on their chins.

Fat tissue under the skin on the face decreases, resulting in wrinkles and sagging skin. Fat tissue often decreases around the eyes so that hollows appear there. Skin on both the underside of the chin and the neck may sag. Sagging also causes the earlobes to lengthen.

A decrease in blood vessels in the superficial layers of the skin results in loss of color. (For all this, however, older people bruise more easily.)

Liver spots, which are brown and flat, may appear on the skin, especially on the backs of hands; they are caused by accumulations of pigment. Raised spots which suddenly appear are not liver spots; they should be brought to the attention of the family physician.

Changes in Vision and Hearing

Eyesight may start to change as early as the fourth decade of life. The ability to see objects at a distance may increase. At some point, the muscles of the eye lose their ability to switch modes from far to near sight. The solution here is bifocals. Also, there is probably some loss of peripheral vision; in this case, people can still clearly perceive objects directly in front of them but not those to the sides.

The size of the pupil of the eye decreases, so less light gets through. This calls for brighter lights for reading and other close work. For instance, in a situation where people in their 20s might need only 20 watts of illumination, people in their 60s might need 40.

Elders may be troubled by dry eyes, caused by the fact that the water content of tears has decreased. Try using lubricating eyedrops.

Some older people have difficulty perceiving contrasts or depths of field. Using contrasting colors for the edges of tables or counters and for the edges of treads on staircases is helpful here.

Hearing loss is usually gradual, and the elder may not realize that it is taking place. Men generally lose their hearing sooner than women do. The first sounds lost are high tones. Consonants may become hard to distinguish; for instance, "pat" and "cat" may sound identical.

If an elder refuses to admit to hearing loss sufficient to cause problems, a referral to an ear, nose and throat specialist from the family physician is in order.

If an elder complains of severe hearing loss experienced over a relatively short period, consult the family physician. The cause is probably a build-up of wax, which the physician will clean out.

Tooth and Mouth Problems

Tooth enamel may become yellow or grayish. If some teeth are missing and dentures are not worn, remaining teeth may move to close gaps.

Gum tissue gradually recedes, exposing the roots of the teeth, and bone sockets around the roots may enlarge. In consequence, teeth may loosen.

The skin covering the lips and mouth may become more fragile; breaks in it may heal more slowly.

Salivary glands may lose some of their effectiveness, possibly resulting in a dry mouth. A dry mouth may cause problems in eating and swallowing, and it may be vulnerable to inflammation and sores. You can buy lubricating preparations to alleviate this problem.

Changes in Nails, Feet and Ankles

Fingernails become thinner and more brittle: keep them cut short and use nail polish (colorless for men) to protect them.

Toenails become thicker and hence more difficult to cut. You may want to call on a podiatrist to do the job.

Calluses and changes in the bone structure of the feet may cause some discomfort, as may loss of fat on the soles of the feet. Again, you may wish to have a podiatrist attend to the problem.

Ankles and feet may swell after prolonged sitting. This is because veins and lymph vessels have become less efficient and are slow to carry fluids away. If ankles and feet swell at all times, not just after prolonged sitting, consult the family physician.

Skin Problems

Sweat glands decrease in number and also produce less sweat. In consequence, skin may become dryer and rougher.

Skin infections may become common. Older people have sensitive skin which may react to bacteria that normally do not penetrate it.

In general, the skin of older people is quick to abrade and form rashes, and it is slow to heal. They should therefore avoid cutting or grazing skin. Bear in mind that they have probably lost much of a protective layer of fat over projecting areas such as elbows, knees and knuckles—and that these areas are particularly susceptible to grazes and cuts.

Changes in Height and Muscle and Fat Tissue

Almost all elders lose some height. Causes are various: decreased size of discs between the vertebrae, stooping, curvature of the spine, slightly bent knees or osteoporosis (bone thinning and loss). If bones break easily, suspect osteoporosis and consult the family physician.

Total muscle mass decreases, resulting in loss of both weight and strength. Exercise can retard loss of muscle mass quite considerably.

The belly may enlarge, due to poor posture, general weakening of the abdominal muscles and/or fat deposits.

Loss of fat tissue on the body may cause bony structures such as the spine, shoulder blades and chest bones to become more prominent. Loss of fat tissue in the breast may also occur.

Reduced Toleration

Because their circulatory system is not as effective as it once was, older people retain heat more than younger people, and do not therefore tolerate heat well. An activity such as mowing the lawn on a hot day, or even just sitting in the sun wearing layers of clothing, may bring on heat exhaustion—which can be fatal. On hot days, check frequently to make sure elders are all right.

By the same token, elders have a lowered resistance to cold and should not spend too much time in cold surroundings or wearing too few clothes on cold days.

To combat both reduced heat and cold tolerance, encourage an elder to wear layered clothing that's easy to put on and take off.

As various bodily functions decline in efficiency, elders' overall reserves are diminished. As a result, their ability to tolerate infectious processes diminishes.

For the same reason, their ability to deal successfully with the side effects of medication, recreational drugs and alcohol diminishes.

Changes in Heart Rate and Oxygen Levels
The heart rate of older people slows down slightly. Note, however, that this does not argue for giving up exercise. For more on exercise, which should be a regular feature of an elder's routine, see Chapter Five.

The level of oxygen in the blood also decreases, but this does not cause shortage of breath. If an elder experiences breathlessness, the cause lies elsewhere, and the family physician should be consulted.

Possible Digestive Problems
Occasionally, acid may back up from the stomach into the oesophagus, causing heartburn. An elder may also have occasional episodes of flatulence, constipation or diarrhea. Note the word "occasional"; if episodes of any of these problems become regular and frequent, consult the family physician.

Reduced Bladder Control
Older people often need to urinate more frequently than younger ones, and may have to get up twice or more during the night to go to the bathroom. To prevent falls, ensure there is a light source with a control by the bed. As well, consider giving an elder the bedroom closest to the bathroom. Alternatively, place a commode in the bedroom or, for men, keep a urinal beside the bed.

Changes in Sexual Performance
Men need a longer stimulation period to achieve an erection. Erections themselves may be less firm, and there will be a decreased volume of semen.

Women experience thinning of the vaginal tissues, which take a longer stimulation period to become lubricated. These changes can make intercourse uncomfortable, if not painful, but artificial lubricants are available to overcome this problem.

Changes in Mental Ability and Functions

The aging of the brain may cause occasional short-term memory loss, such as, "Now where did I put my keys when we came in?" This is because an elder takes more time than a younger person needs to access a short-term memory. Note that this is quite different from dementias such as Alzheimers. In due course, the healthy elder will remember where the keys are; for someone with dementia that memory is gone forever.

Here's More Help

Healthy Happy Aging: A Positive Approach to Active Living, by Yvonne Wagorn, Sonia Theberge and Dr. William A.R. Orban, has chapters on how the body ages, living with aging, and common physical disorders. It also has several chapters on exercise, a topic dealt with in Chapter Five. It is obtainable from General Store Publishing House Inc., 1 Main St., Burnstown, Ont., K0J 1G0, for $20 plus $4 for shipping, handling and GST.

How We Die: Reflections on Life's Final Chapter, by Sherwin B. Nuland, explores some of the conditions of later life that can lead to death, among them cancer, heart attack, Alzheimers and stroke. Published by Random House of Canada, it is available in bookstores across the country in paperback for $17.95.

Ourselves Growing Older: Women Aging with Knowledge and Power, by Paula B. Doress-Worters and Diana Laskin Siegal, has chapters on changes associated with aging and on conditions associated with aging such as diabetes, hypertension and osteoporosis, as well as on subjects relevant to other chapters in this book. Published by Simon & Schuster, it is available in bookstores across Canada for $23.

Hume Medical Information Services has produced six video-and-manual packages on high blood pressure, arthritis, angina and heart disease, migraine headaches, diabetes and asthma respectively. The videos run anywhere from 28 to 35 minutes, and the manuals have 128 pages. The packages are available from most large drugstores in Canada and the U.S. or direct from Hume at 160 Bloor St. E., Toronto, M4W 1B9. The suggested list price is $29.95, but some outlets have charged $34.95, while others have had the package on special at $19.95.

Medical Audio Visual Communications to date has produced 35 videos featuring Dr. Rob Buckman and John Cleese on subjects ranging from depression and osteoarthritis to enlarged prostate and chronic bronchitis and emphysema. Videos last anywhere from 23 minutes to more than 60 minutes. For a catalogue, call the company toll-free at 1-800-757-4868. The videos are available from the company at P.O. Box 84548, 2336 Bloor St. W., Toronto, M6S 1T0, for $99, plus $6 for shipping and handling, plus taxes.

Eldercare is a 12-page newsletter for caregivers, published six times a year, containing information relevant to the subjects of many chapters in this book. To subscribe, send $19.80 ($18.50 + $1.30 GST) to Eldercare, 12 Donora Drive, Suite 202, Toronto, M4B 1B4.

CHAPTER FIVE

Health Check and Health Care

Anyone who believes older people inevitably become decrepit and enfeebled in their later years would do well to heed the examples set by two American women, Donietta Bickley and Kiki David.

At the age of 80, Donietta, a native of Baltimore, Maryland, had competed in—and completed—six marathons. Kiki, a native of Ann Arbor, Michigan, had also completed six marathons—at the age of 91.

Such accomplishments call for considerable advance preparation, of course. The news item that introduced me to Donietta pointed out that she ran 50 miles each week, walked and swam on a regular basis, and also enjoyed aerobics, line dancing and tennis. Furthermore, she had been a physically active person all her adult life. Kiki's training was described as no less rigorous and varied; she was covering up to eight miles per day running, then walking, then running some more, and she also did aerobics exercises, weightlifted, rode a stationary bicycle and swam.

I learned about these two veteran marathoners in the pages of *Optimum*, the newsletter of the Institute for Positive Health for

Seniors, a publication that contains much useful information for people who want to age well. (You'll learn how to subscribe to *Optimum* later in this chapter.)

Appropriate exercise is just one aspect of health maintenance in later life. We'll examine it and other aspects in this chapter. We'll also look at some health tips and at regular health checks a care receiver or his or her caregiver should perform.

Health Maintenance

To maintain health in later life, three things are of paramount importance: exercising appropriately, eating and drinking healthy foods and liquids and making sure that medications are taken in the right quantity and at the right time. Let's now take a brief look at all three.

Exercise

You don't have to look far in the press to find reports of benefits elders experience after taking up exercise programs. Here, for instance, is one concerning a group of women aged 50 to 70, some of whom did two 45-minute exercise programs a week. At the end of one year, the exercising members of the group improved their strength and balance and—no less important—experienced increased bone mass. Here's another report concerning 100 nursing home residents, average age 87. Half of them worked out with weights for 45 minutes three times a week while the others did not. At the end of 10 weeks, those who exercised were found to have increased their walking speed and their power to climb stairs, due to increased muscle strength and tone. They also walked more often and had fewer balance problems than before.

An ideal exercise program has four components: warmup and stretch, calisthenics, aerobics, cool down and stretch. Here are the reasons.

Warming up and cooling down are essentials. Nobody, not even younger people, should go full tilt into an energetic workout. The rule is: start slowly, then speed up, then tail off. Stretching is good because it improves posture and increases flexibility.

Calisthenic exercises, such as working out with weights, increase muscle strength and endurance, as well as firming and toning muscle tissues.

Aerobic exercises, such as swimming, fast walking or working out on a stationary bicycle, treadmill or stairclimber, raise the heart rate, increase oxygen intake levels, improve breathing ability and generally make for a healthy heart and help to reduce the risk of cardiovascular disease. Aerobic exercise is also beneficial for anyone experiencing a mild depression; it causes the brain to release natural antidepressant chemicals called endorphins.

For most elders, swimming and walking are the best forms of aerobic exercise.

Swimming is great exercise. A swimmer floating in water is at virtually no risk of straining muscles—which is emphatically not the case for a runner. Swimming tones the muscles, helps keep both heart and lungs in good shape and helps elders lose weight.

An elder just beginning a swimming program should start small and work up: begin maybe with a 15-minute swim twice a week, and work up to 20- to 30-minute swims four or five times a week. If swimming is the exercise of choice, this person needs a sensible swimsuit rather than a decorative one, and a pair of goggles.

Walking does good in many ways. Walkers, who should use a waist pack instead of a purse so that their arms swing freely, are ensuring their leg and arm muscles remain healthy. They are giving their cardiovascular system a good workout. And, if they walk relatively vigorously and often, they may help prevent osteoporosis (loss of bone mass).

However, if an elder has already developed osteoporosis, he or she should check with the family physician before embarking on a walking regimen—or any exercise program—to make sure the activity proposed is safe.

Walking may also help to lower the level of undesirable triglycerides in the bloodstream. One group of researchers studied a group of men and women who walked for two hours and another group who were not active. Each group was then fed a meal with a high fat content. The walkers had triglyceride levels almost one-third lower than those who had not walked.

No one yet knows why, but older people who walk are far less likely to suffer severe gastrointestinal bleeding than are elderly couch potatoes. (Gastrointestinal bleeding, which can be fatal, is by no means uncommon among the elderly.)

When walking, an older person should limber up by doing some stretching exercises first, then warm up by walking slowly for the first five minutes. Then speed up to a regular pace, slowing down again for the final five minutes.

If your care receiver lives near a large mall, ask mall staff whether there is a walkers' group there. They exist in many malls, and most walk early in the day before stores open. Some are totally informal—just a bunch of people who came to the common realization that, with its level ground, equable climate, and well-lit safety, a mall is a great place to get fit by walking. Other mall walking groups are far more formal, with registration, and perhaps even uniform T-shirts or other garb.

Incidentally, an elder's choice of exercise is indicative of her or his personality. An extrovert will enjoy the companionship of others as she walks in the mall. An introvert will thoroughly enjoy his daily swim by himself. And enjoyment of the chosen exercise form is essential because the exerciser will participate with energy bred of enthusiasm, and will not be tempted to quit because "this is not fun."

Your care receiver enjoys other physical activities? So much the better. You should know that 20 minutes of vigorous ballroom dancing or 36 minutes spent pushing a power lawn mower provides as good a workout as 20 minutes of running, and that 30 minutes of raking leaves equals 20 minutes of aerobic exercises.

Mental Exercise

Just as retreating physically from the world and becoming chair-bound and inactive does not bode well for physical health in later life, shutting oneself away mentally and ceasing to have contact with mentally active people does not bode well for mental health. Curiosity is not the preserve only of young people; it is a mental tonic throughout life.

Studies have shown that those who have a high degree of verbal fluency or an above-average level of ability in reading comprehension and those who retain keen mental interests in later life are likely to enjoy good mental function in old age. A desire to learn new things and to experience change are also good signs.

Mental acumen rubs off. An older person living with or in frequent contact with someone who is challenging him or her may benefit by enjoying increased mental activity. Grandchildren may enjoy participating in this way. Playing an elder at Scrabble, chess or Trivial Pursuit is fun and great mental exercise. So is doing cryptic crosswords together.

Diet

Elderly people often don't eat well. If your care receiver doesn't live with you, find some way to check what kind of food and drink she or he is ingesting.

One quite common situation is that of an elder who has dental problems and who stops eating certain foods important to a balanced diet because they are hard to chew. The solution here may be a dental appointment. Or it may be to prepare foods differently—serving vegetables cooked rather than raw in a salad, or cooking them longer so that they are more tender.

Elderly people who eat alone are at greatest risk of malnutrition. Lacking someone to enjoy a meal with, they either don't bother to eat regularly and snack instead of having a meal, or they may miss a meal entirely. They may also give in to a craving for unhealthy foods. (Bear in mind that an overweight person can just as easily be malnourished as a thin one.)

If your care receiver has no companion to share a meal with, consider whether you could have a meal with him or her once daily or at least several times a week. Perhaps he or she could come to your house for dinner, for instance.

Another alternative is Meals on Wheels. Many elders won't take Meals on Wheels, believing the mass-prepared food will be dull. Here's a plan of action you could try. Order up Meals on Wheels on a temporary basis, without telling your care receiver that you have done so. Be there when the first meal delivery takes place so he or she doesn't tell the deliverer to take the food away. Try the food yourself, saying, "Hey, this is good! Have some." In most cases, curiosity will get the better of the elder.

You should be aware that some elders develop a form of anorexia (starving oneself due to lack of appetite). Unlike anorexia nervosa, the condition suffered by young women, this type may be caused by loneliness, illness, stress, depression or dementia. As well, some medications reduce the appetite, while others cause stomach upsets so that the user reduces food intake to a minimum. If you suspect the latter, list all the medications this person takes and consult a pharmacist. In all cases, if you think this person has anorexia, consult the family physician, who may provide a referral to a psychiatrist or a nutritionist.

Lack of certain substances in the diet can have strange effects. For instance, if you notice that your care receiver seems to be confused or appears to be undergoing some kind of personality change, this may be caused by too little sugar in the diet. Marked irritability, depression or even slight dementia may be symptoms of anemia. If you see any of these symptoms, consult the family physician, who may provide a referral to a nutritionist.

The biggest dietary mistake many people make is eating a tiny breakfast or none at all, and having a large dinner in the evening. In the morning, the body needs fuel to get through the day ahead. In the evening, it needs very little because it is winding down. The healthier pattern is a large breakfast, a smaller lunch and an even smaller supper, with a healthy snack in the middle of the morning and the middle of the afternoon.

What might constitute a healthy snack? Sunflower seeds, dried apricots, vegetable sticks or a piece of fresh fruit, to name just a few.

As people age, they often have lower energy levels and hence need fewer calories. But they need no fewer nutrients than younger people—and indeed they may need more if their bodies aren't able to absorb nutrients as efficiently as they once did. For this reason, be sure your care receiver is following the recommendations set out in Canada's Food Guide in terms of daily intake: five to 10 servings of fruit and vegetables, five to 12 servings of grain products, two to four servings of milk and milk products, and two to three servings of meat, fish, poultry and alternates. (Among alternates you might consider are beans, tofu, lentils, eggs and peanut butter.)

Medications

Among the elderly, one in five hospital admissions is due to medications—either overmedication, improper mixing of medications or problematic side effects. Even more dramatic, bad reactions to drugs are the reason for almost half of the visits made to hospitals' emergency departments by elderly women.

There are good reasons for these remarkable statistics. New drugs are tested on young people but often dispensed to elderly people whose reaction to them may be far stronger. In the same vein, new drugs are often tested on men, but often prescribed for women who, with smaller bodies, may need smaller dosages.

There are proven ways to keep out of trouble with drugs.

You and your care receiver should tell the family physician that you both want to take as few drugs as possible. If the physician doesn't listen and prescribes a whole raft of medications without explaining why they are necessary, consider shopping for another physician.

If prescribed drugs produce side effects other than those the prescribing physician has mentioned as a likely consequence of taking them, report this immediately to the physician.

Anyone on prescription medication should not take nonprescription or over-the-counter (OTC) drugs without first obtaining the assurance of either the prescribing physician or a pharmacist that the combination is not harmful.

Don't take any drugs that are unlabeled or have expired. If you find any which have expired, or which have been discontinued—perhaps because they caused severe side effects—take them to your pharmacy for safe disposal.

Don't mix drugs with alcohol.

Don't use medications prescribed for someone else.

If you forget to take a dose, don't double up when you are due to take the next dose. Call your pharmacist for advice.

Don't keep sedatives at the bedside. Someone fogged with sleep may take them by mistake.

Keep medications in a dry, dark place. Don't keep them in the bathroom; both moisture and heat may damage them. Keep them in the refrigerator only if specifically told to do so.

Be aware that anyone who takes mood-altering drugs—anti-depressants, sleeping pills or tranquilizers—can easily become dependent on them. For instance, anyone who takes two or three tranquilizers a day can develop a dependency on them after about a month. Similarly, anyone who takes one sleeping pill every night for a month can become dependent on them. Older women are particularly susceptible in this regard. Most important of all, patronize only one pharmacy and make sure the pharmacist keeps your personal profile on computer. That way, she or he will notice immediately if a newly prescribed drug will interact badly with another medication being taken. If you take OTC drugs, tell the pharmacist about these too so that your profile will be complete.

Elderly people are more likely than younger ones to experience side effects from medications. Some side effects are quite bizarre. For instance, if your care receiver is on medications and develops blurred vision, eye dryness, yellow-tinged vision, red spots on the surface of the eye or a change in the size of the pupil, consult a pharmacist or the prescribing physician. By the same token, seek professional guidance if an elder on a new medication suddenly starts having episodes of confusion or disorientation, losing coordination, falling or experiencing nausea.

Health Tips

Medication Know-how

You or your care receiver should keep a record of all medications your care receiver takes. The record should show the drugs' names and the reason for their use. It should also show how and at what time of the day the drugs should be taken. If your care receiver is taking a variety of medications and could become confused, the record might also indicate what each drug looks like—"yellow round tablet" for instance, or "blue-and-white capsule." This description should be checked when a new prescription has been filled in case the pharmacist has used a different brand of the drug which does not answer to the noted description. If a drug causes side effects, these should also be noted.

This record will furnish useful information for your care receiver's family physician. And if the elder makes a note every time a drug is taken, it will prevent accidental double-dosing.

If pills or capsules are small or slippery and hence difficult for elderly—and possibly arthritic—hands to grasp, put them in an eggcup or demitasse. Now the user simply tosses the container back as if drinking a liquid.

If elderly hands have trouble getting childproof caps off pill containers, ask the pharmacist to give you an easily opened container. Use this to store the medication—and keep it somewhere out of the reach of children.

If your care receiver takes sublingual (placed under the tongue) or buccal (placed in the cheek pocket) drugs, she or he should rinse the mouth with water first. A clean mouth helps the body to absorb drugs more easily and faster.

Pills will go down more easily if the user swallows a mouthful of water before taking them and several mouthfuls afterwards. If the user stands up and does not tilt his or her head back, this will also make swallowing easier.

A pill lodged in the throat can irritate the oesophagus and even ulcerate it. The person with this problem should sit upright and relax as much as possible, while taking a few sips of a carbonated drink—or water, if a carbonated drink is not available. After 15 minutes, if the pill is still stuck, call the family physician for advice. After 30 minutes, if it still has not gone down, go to a hospital emergency department. However, the last two steps are seldom needed, since relaxation combined with the carbonated drink usually solves the problem.

If liquid medicine is bitter-tasting, the user should hold her or his nose. If tablets are bitter-tasting, the user should put them on the front of the tongue. The tastebuds at the back of the tongue detect bitterness, while those at the front detect sweetness.

If your care receiver doesn't want to take medications, or perhaps chokes while trying to swallow pills, ask the pharmacist whether you may grind the pills up into powder form (many pills must not be crushed) and, if the pharmacist gives you the go-ahead, mix the powder with some soft food the user likes—jam or jelly, for instance.

If pills must be cut in half, doing the job with a knife may cause them to crumble, hence making it difficult to get an accurate dose. Most pharmacies sell inexpensive plastic pill cutters, which do the job neatly.

If your care receiver must take pills while in bed, he or she should sit up, drink a whole glassful of water after swallowing the pills, and remain upright until the pills have gone right down.

Some medications cause users' mouths to feel dry. If your care receiver is on such a medication, ask the pharmacist for a saliva substitute. Your care receiver should also not use any mouthwash containing alcohol, since this may also cause a dry mouth. A pharmacist will be able to recommend a fluoride rinse.

If your care receiver must take a variety of drugs on a daily basis, consider buying a daily pill dispenser to ensure that the right dosages are taken. Pharmacies usually stock several kinds, most of which hold a week's supply of medications.

If your care receiver has poor eyesight and has trouble distinguishing among pill containers, several remedies exist. If the user has difficulty deciphering the small print on labels, ask the pharmacist for either a label or a separate sheet of instructions typed in large print. If the user can still distinguish colors clearly, wrap brightly colored tapes around medication containers or paint their caps, and make sure the user knows that blue signifies an arthritis remedy and red a diabetes one or whatever.

Dental Know-how

If your care receiver has trouble holding a regular toothbrush firmly, look for special brushes at your local pharmacy; they usually have enlarged and/or angled handles. Or you could enlarge the handle of a regular toothbrush by making a hole in a small rubber ball and slipping the ball over the handle. Slipping a bicycle handle grip over the toothbrush handle serves the same purpose, as does enlarging the handle by wrapping it in several layers of masking tape.

If flossing has become difficult for elderly hands, use a plastic flossholder, available at pharmacies. Flossing, which may be done either before or after brushing, must not be abandoned; anyone who doesn't floss is not cleaning a full 35% of each tooth surface.

Consider buying an electric toothbrush for your care receiver. It has a far thicker handle than a regular brush and it is also heavier, both of which make grasping it firmly easier. Ask a dental hygienist to recommend a brand. Or make sure the one you choose has an on/off switch that starts automatically with pressure, a circular up-and-down bristle motion and soft nylon bristles.

When cleaning dentures, put a facecloth in the basin. If the denture is dropped, the facecloth will cushion the fall.

To make cleaning dentures easier, attach suction cups to a denture brush to affix it to a vanity top or adjacent wall. The user then rubs the dentures across the brush to clean them.

Ill-fitting dentures or ones that are not cleaned regularly can cause inflammation and lesions. Their wearer will experience discomfort and may have problems both eating and speaking. Since older people often don't like changing to a new set of dentures, the solution to ill-fitting ones is usually to reline or repair them as necessary.

Eyedrop and Eardrop Know-how

When you put drops in your care receiver's eyes, ask her or him to blink as little as possible. Blinking causes the drops to drain out of the eye more quickly.

Another way to prevent the drops from draining out too fast is to close the user's eye and, using a tissue, exert gentle pressure on the corner of the eye nearest the nose for a minute or two. This action blocks the tear duct and so helps keep the medication in the eye.

Eyedrops should be dropped onto the inside of the lower lid, not directly onto the eyeball. Eye ointment should be applied in a similar manner.

To raise the temperature of eardrops to a comfortable level, hold the container in your hands for a few minutes. Or run tepid—but not hot—water over the container for a minute or two.

Do not drop eardrops straight down the ear. Instead, dribble them onto the side of the ear canal.

Health Check

You should make sure your care receiver has regular professional health checks. For instance, an annual checkup by the family physician is a must. The physician may refer the patient to a laboratory for blood and urine tests and/or an electrocardiogram (it checks the condition of the heart).

If the patient is female, a breast examination, pap smear and mammogram will probably be part of the annual checkup. If the patient is male, the checkup will likely include a testicular and prostate examination.

Your care receiver should have a dental checkup twice a year (unless she or he has no natural teeth). She or he should also see an opthalmologist at least once a year to check for vision change and the beginning of glaucoma or cataracts, or to monitor existing conditions.

Now here are some regular checks that you or your care receiver should carry out.

Skin Check

Have your care receiver check for dry patches of skin—or do it yourself if you bathe him or her. As you'll recall from Chapter Four, elders' sweat glands decrease and this can lead to dry skin. Use a good moisturizer: your family physician can probably recommend one. Or go the inexpensive and no less effective route—use baby oil.

The elderly are especially prone to fungal infections. As well as checking between the toes—see **Foot Alert**, on the next page—the groin, underarms, fingernails and toenails, the soles and sides of the feet, and the heels should be checked regularly. The presence of any unusual signs—skin abrasion, blistering, extreme skin dryness, redness or other discoloration, for instance—calls for a visit to the family physician.

If you notice any changes in a mole or wart, or a sore that doesn't heal, consult the family physician without delay.

Bedsore Alert

If this person spends much time in bed, check the skin often for the beginning of bedsores. You're most likely to find the slight redness that signals poor circulation—the root cause of bedsores—on shoulder blades, elbows, the base of the spine, hips, buttocks and the backs of heels. If this person lies often on one side or the other, check the sides of shoulders, elbows and ankles. A bedsore may also start on the back of the head, but this happens only rarely. You'll find information on how to prevent bedsores from developing in Chapter Ten.

Anemia Check

If you notice an unusual skin pallor and/or if fingernail beds become very pale and almost white, this person may have become anemic.

As a double check, pull the lower eyelid down and check the color of its inner side. It should be a healthy pink. If it is pale—again, almost white—here is another indication of anemia.

Anemia can be highly debilitating, especially if it goes untreated for quite a while. If you see the above signs, this person should consult with the family physician.

Scalp and Hair Examination

You should inspect your care receiver's scalp regularly at hairwashing time. You are looking for sores or dandruff. Baby oil applied before shampooing will soothe sores, and dandruff will probably respond to the use of a medicated shampoo. However, if any of these conditions seems serious or persists despite your best efforts, consult the family physician.

Also check regularly for lice or nits. If you find them, use a shampoo containing gamma benzene hexachloride or one containing permethrin, and comb with a special nit comb—it has especially fine teeth—to remove the parasites' eggs.

If hair suddenly becomes dry and brittle and/or if it starts thinning markedly, this person may have a serious hormonal imbalance or a diminished ability to absorb nutrients. Stress and poor dietary habits can also cause hair dryness and loss. Don't ignore these changes; this person should see the family physician.

Foot Alert

When checking the feet for fungal infections, also check for calluses, corns and ingrown or overgrown toenails. If any of these are present, your care receiver should seek professional help from a podiatrist.

The feet of an elder who has diabetes should be checked on a daily basis. People who have diabetes are more susceptible to foot problems than most people. Diabetes causes a loss of sensation in the feet, so sufferers may not notice a skin abrasion or the beginning of an ulcer. And, due to poor circulation caused by diabetes, an ulcerative condition can quickly turn gangrenous if it is not found and treated promptly.

If the daily foot check of a person with diabetes reveals any irregularity or change, consult a podiatrist or the family physician immediately.

Mouth Check

Your care receiver's mouth should be checked regularly—twice a month perhaps, or right away if he or she complains of discomfort—for signs of trouble. If you find oozing pus along the gum line, the cause could be an abcess or some other infection. Check thoroughly for swellings, white or red patches or any gum discoloration, blisters or sores that don't heal in a few days. If he or she wears dentures, look for reddened areas or inflammation beneath them; this may indicate that the dentures do not fit well. If you find any of these conditions, your care receiver should see a dentist or a physician.

However, sores under dentures can also be caused by tiny fragments of nut or berry or fig pips that have worked their way under the denture and been forced into the flesh by the act of chewing. After eating any foods that might cause this problem, the wearer should remove and clean the denture and rinse the mouth.

If your care receiver complains of a dry mouth, she or he should rinse it out. Or you can use swab sticks bought at a pharmacy and dipped in a solution of a teaspoon of salt or baking soda dissolved in a quart of warm water. Dentures should be removed before swabbing.

If this person continues to complain of a dry mouth after rinsing or swabbing, ask a pharmacist for an artificial saliva preparation.

If the tongue has a thick coating, this may indicate dehydration. Remove the coating, using gauze soaked in a 50:50 mixture of water and hydrogen peroxide. (This mixture should not be swallowed.) Make sure your care receiver increases fluid intake—we should all drink the equivalent of six to eight tumblers of fluid a day, of which four or more should be water. If the coating returns after this person's fluid intake has been normalized for a week or so, consult the family physician.

Eye Alert

If your care receiver's eyes look pink or sore, ask if they feel sore. If the answer is in the affirmative, the eyes should be bathed, using either previously boiled tepid water or a solution made by dissolving one teaspoonful of boracic acid in a pint of previously boiled tepid water, and cotton swabs, which you can buy at a pharmacy. Swab the eyes from the nose outward, and use each swab only once.

If the soreness persists despite this treatment, you should make an appointment with the family physician.

Clot Watch

If your care receiver complains of pain in a leg, and if you gently check the location of the pain and find swelling, redness or heat there, a blood clot may have formed. Consult the family physician right away, and do not under any circumstances rub the affected area; if you do so, you may dislodge the clot or break it up, in which case it could travel to the brain, lungs or heart, where it could cause a stroke, a heart attack or even death.

Urine and Stool Examination

Check—or ask your care receiver to check—the color of urine passed on a daily basis. Urine should be clear, of the consistency of water and the color of pale straw. If it is darker, this could suggest dehydration; make sure this person drinks plenty of fluids, among them water. If the urine is milky and thick, consult the family physician; an infection may be present. If there is blood in the urine, it will have a pinkish or reddish tinge. However, some medications can change the color of urine so, before panicking and rushing off to the family physician, list all the medications this person is taking and talk to a pharmacist. Pink-tinged urine can also result from eating certain foods, among them beetroots.

Stools should also be checked regularly. A healthy stool is soft and fairly pale brown. If stools become dark brown, or blackish with a sticky consistency, or hard, a visit to the family physician is in order. Again, be aware that some foods and medications can change the color of stools.

If any blood is found in the toilet bowl or on toilet paper, again consult the family physician, even if you know or believe the cause to be hemorrhoids.

Cancer Alert

Sores that won't heal, changes in the appearance of a wart or mole, and traces of blood in the urine or stool may all indicate the presence of a malignancy and, as noted above, should be reported to the family physician without delay.

Here are some other symptoms that may indicate the presence of a malignancy: a change in the frequency of bowel movements, persistent constipation, diarrhea (unless accompanied by other symptoms of gastric flu), persistent stomach discomfort or indigestion, a persistent sore throat or nagging cough, difficulty in swallowing, difficulty in breathing, blood in the sputum, a thickening or lump in any part of the body, difficulty in urinating or defecating, persistent pain that has no apparent cause in any part of the body. All these symptoms can indicate the presence of some disorder other than cancer, but take no chances and make an appointment with the family physician immediately in all cases.

Difficulties in Diagnosing Mental Problems

If you think you detect signs of dementia in an elder, don't jump to conclusions. Symptoms similar to those of dementia can be caused by depression, loss of hearing or sight or a chemical imbalance of some kind. They can also be caused by medications, so your first step should be to consult a pharmacist, taking with you a list of medications this person takes. If the pharmacist tells you the medications are not the cause, consult the family physician.

Mood-altering medications—a blanket term for tranquilizers, sleeping pills and antidepressants, among other substances—can cause their users to experience depression, anxiety or confusion, even when taken in small quantities. If your care receiver is prescribed a mood-altering medication and becomes depressed, anxious or confused, consult the family physician, who may be able to prescribe medications that do not have these side effects.

If your care receiver complains of loss of energy, insomnia, anxiety, changes in weight and/or appetite or problems digesting food, she or he may actually be suffering from depression, especially if more than one of these complaints is cited. Other symptoms of depression? Feelings of irritability or sadness; loss of interest in activities once enjoyed; inability to concentrate, remember things or make decisions; restlessness or decreased activity; feelings of guilt, hopelessness or worthlessness; changes in sleep patterns; hostility; pessimism; thoughts of death or suicide. In all cases, consult the family physician, who will first ascertain whether there are any physical causes for these changes and, if no such causes are found, will probably refer this person to a geriatric psychiatrist.

Assistive Devices

If your care receiver uses a hearing aid but seems to be becoming deaf all over again, first check out the aid's batteries. If they are not exhausted, have the aid checked out by the company from which it was bought. If the company finds that the aid is not malfunctioning, consult the family physician; the problem may be a build up of ear wax.

Check the tips of any canes your care receiver uses. If the rubber tip is worn thin—or perhaps worn right through—affix a new tip.

Check any glasses worn to make sure all screws are tight. If any are loose, the lenses could fall out or the sidepieces could come off. If you find loose screws, take the glasses back to the optician from whom they were bought. Staff at the store will fix the problem screws permanently, almost certainly without charge.

Remember that wheelchairs of all types and motorized scooters must be serviced at regular intervals as specified in their manuals if they are to remain in good working order.

Here's More Help

As mentioned earlier in this chapter, *Optimum* is a good source of information and counsel on aging well. The newsletter is published by the Institute for Positive Health for Seniors. To receive a copy of the latest issue, write to the institute at 43 Bruyere St., Ottawa, K1N 5C8, enclosing $2 to cover mailing and handling charges.

The institute also has a procedure that physically tests the energy level of elders. It is universal and measures the energy change in an elder while performing simple exercises. Other than a weight scale, a stopwatch and a measuring tape, the only tools you need are one or two flights of stairs, a wall for wall push-ups and a straight 60-foot unobstructed space for fast walking. Test procedures are available from the institute at the above address for $5 a set.

Former ballet dancer Lilian Jarvis, who is 64 but looks perhaps 44, has developed an exercise system that she calls BioSomatics, whose only prop is a length of soft fabric. Her book, *Stress Releaser Stretchcloth*, comes packaged with a stretchcloth. It is published by Moulin Publishing and costs $22.95. To order a copy, or to find out more about BioSomatics, call the publisher toll-free at 1-800-489-8715.

The Heart and Stroke Foundation has literature on exercising and nutrition. Contact the regional office nearest to you.

It Works for Us! A Guide to Healthful Eating for Older Adults is a 28-page booklet full of useful information and advice. It is available without charge from the Metropolitan Toronto Chapter, Canadian Pensioners Concerned, 51 Bond St., Toronto, M5B 1X1.

CHAPTER SIX

Effective New Age Elderhelp

People with Alzheimers are often a source of great worry to their caregivers, not least because they roam and, forgetting where they live, fail to come home. However, Earl Flemming, 65, who lives in Spryfield, a suburb of Halifax, is no source of worry to his 59-year-old caregiver wife, Peggy, on this score.

"He won't leave because of the dog," she says contentedly. "I don't think anyone who came into the house to help me do anything, even take care of him, would take the dog's place. The dog even comes before me, I think!"

If you ask Peggy whether the dog has been a boon to Earl since he developed Alzheimers, she replies, "Yes—oh my God yes! I think there would have been days when he wouldn't have gotten up out of bed if he hadn't had the dog." As it is, Earl gets up at about 7:30 a.m., goes downstairs—the Flemmings have a second-floor apartment—takes the dog out and hooks him up to his line, makes a big fuss over him, comes back indoors to mix some dog food and takes it down to him. Instead of feeding him immediately, Earl pretends he is going to eat the food himself.

"He has done this since the dog was a pup," Peggy explains. "Now the dog won't eat unless he's teased."

All through the day, she says, Earl will look out to make sure the dog is all right. He takes down water for him now and then, and feeds him again at four o'clock. "He remembers the ritual—more so than using deodorant or having a bath.

"Oh, and he loves the cats too. Toffee follows Earl around like a puppy dog. If he isn't around, Earl will go and look for him."

Pet-Facilitated Therapy, or PFT, is just one form of alternative elder-help that has been found highly effective in helping to keep older people in good physical and mental health, and generally to help fill their days. As a caregiver, you should ensure that your care receiver is able to pursue some enjoyable activity for as long as she or he is capable of doing so. Perhaps you have at one time or another been in a nursing home where the residents sit motionless in rows, having not been encouraged into some kind of activity. You surely would not want your care receiver to sit still, staring into space, for hours on end.

Activities many elders enjoy include knitting, sewing, drawing, painting, reading and playing games. In this chapter, we'll take a close look at 10 therapeutic activities, among them PFT. This list is by no means exhaustive. For instance, social therapy is not covered. This describes the activities of a group of older people who meet regularly, sometimes for a specific reason (perhaps they have all been recently widowed and are sharing their knowledge about how to cope with bereavement) or just to socialize. Studies have shown that people who belong to self-help groups cope better with chronic conditions of ill-health than those who do not belong.

Incidentally, while these activities are often referred to as therapies, this is something of a misnomer since, strictly speaking, a therapy is a treatment of a disorder, while these activities are normally engaged in by healthy people. They might best be described as enhancements of the quality of life. However, since their practitioners refer to them as therapies, I'll continue to use the term, bearing in mind all the while that these are "feel-better therapies," not "get-better therapies."

Pet-Facilitated Therapy

Many thousands of older Canadians have used and enjoyed PFT. Its benefits have proven to be several and almost immediate. For instance, anyone with high blood pressure who pets an animal will probably experience lowered pressure within minutes. People with pets are also generally more contented than those without pets. And, since pets—like the weather—are a surefire conversation opener, even with strangers, pet owners tend to be more outgoing and to enjoy better social interaction.

Having a pet brings another benefit. As they become less able to perform a full range of activities, elders often find they have to hand over responsibilities to caregivers. Owning a pet means being responsible for that pet, and people enjoy this aspect of the relationship.

If you want to obtain a pet for your care receiver, you might contact the local branch of the Society for the Prevention of Cruelty to Animals or your local humane society. Either may offer a service matching pets to people. If your care receiver is frail and can move only with difficulty, she or he will be best paired to a mature, trained pet, not to a frisky kitten or puppy.

There is a potential down side to acquiring a pet for your care receiver. If she or he isn't capable of looking after it—feeding, grooming, exercising and so on—you may end up being a caregiver to the pet too.

Looking Good

People of all ages—and elders are no exception—feel better about themselves when they are well dressed and tidy. Looking good is indeed a therapy of sorts.

If your care receiver is freshly shaved and dressed in a clean shirt and pullover, he'll feel far more cheerful than he would if you hadn't shaved him and had left him in his rumpled pyjamas.

Elderly women accustomed to wearing makeup don't feel fully dressed without it—and makeup can help to hide some of the effects of aging, such as dark circles under the eyes or broken blood vessels. Many of them also greatly enjoy wearing nail polish for the first time in their lives. It's a signal that they have finally become "ladies of leisure."

Music Therapy

David Loyst, a registered music therapist working at Riverdale Hospital in Toronto, tells of an occasion when music became a bridge over a chasm of noncommunication between a patient and his helpers.

The patient had terminal cancer. He was uncommunicative, and staff at the hospital found him difficult. "He was not the easiest sort of person to like on the surface," Loyst recalls. One day, Loyst asked him if he had ever played music, and he said he had been a member of a marching band as a kid. He said he liked marches, so Loyst brought him in some march music. The patient clearly enjoyed it, and became slightly more communicative. Then Loyst asked if he had a favorite song, and he said he had one he couldn't get out of his mind, called "Help Me Make It Through the Night." Loyst took the music in to the hospital, and sang the song to him. The words of the chorus were "Yesterdays are dead and gone/ And tomorrow is out of sight/ Oh it's sad to be alone/ Help me make it through the night."

Loyst asked him if these words meant anything particular to him.

He replied, "Yesterdays are dead and gone, sometimes we do wrong things." Loyst realized that the patient was coming to terms with some guilt feelings. He then asked what the second line meant to him. The patient said, "Well, I don't know how many days I have left." Asked about the third line, he said no, he didn't feel alone any more because Loyst and the chaplain came to see him often and the staff were all so nice to him. And so far as the last line was concerned, he said he hoped he would die in his sleep. From then on, the patient was pleasant and more talkative, and highly appreciative of all that staff and volunteers did for him.

Music used as therapy can do far more than open up channels of communication. If you listen to music that you enjoy, your body will produce a greater flow of endorphins, which are natural painkillers. Hence music can be seen as a painkiller. Soothing music—instrumental is better than vocal, since words may be distracting—can lower blood pressure, produce slower, deeper breathing and improve the functioning of the gastrointestinal system.

As well, as Loyst points out, people listening to rhythmic music find they have more freedom of movement and are able to move more fluidly. This can be a great help to people with Parkinsons, who have difficulty in moving smoothly because their muscles are in tension. (Some music therapists also encourage people with Parkinsons to sing because quite often they can sing more clearly than they can speak, which is a great morale booster for them. As well, singing vigorously improves breathing.) It could also be helpful to people whose freedom of movement has been impaired by a mild stroke.

Loyst works often with patients who have dementia. "I find music can help me tap into their long-term memories by using some songs that were popular during their youth." Some of these patients, who probably can't recall having had breakfast an hour ago, are able to sing several verses of an old favorite. "Musical memory seems to be quite resilient, even in people with a lot of neurological damage such as from a stroke or from Alzheimers," Loyst says.

Increasingly, hospitals are providing patients with tapes to alleviate their anxiety and pain before, during and after surgery. And the patients aren't the only ones being helped by music. Surgeons find they work better if suitable music is piped into the operating room.

Music is also used in retirement homes as a means of breaking down isolation and shyness. Music that was popular in the residents' youth brings to mind happy memories and residents often start sharing these memories with those around them. This use of music needn't be restricted to institutional settings: if your elderly parents are entertaining other elderly people, playing music that was popular when they were all young will probably be a happy experience, provoking lively conversation.

What kind of music is most therapeutic? This depends on whether its function is to sedate or stimulate listeners. Loyst uses music played on a harp, violin, piano or guitar for a sedative effect. It should not be too loud, and it should be slow: if it has more than 60 beats per minute, or one beat per second, it will speed up the heartbeat. If a stimulus is required—perhaps to exercise more vigorously—faster music played on brass instruments with drum accompaniment is more appropriate.

Clearly, if your care receiver doesn't like music or is highly sensitive to sounds, she or he is unlikely to find music therapeutic.

A final thought on music therapy. People often ask David Loyst, "What should I listen to in order to relax?" There is no one single right answer. If your care receiver likes Beethoven sonatas and Rita MacNeil, that might be his or her choice. If your care receiver detests classical music and female vocalists, neither Ludwig nor Rita will provide relaxation.

Sounds of Serenity

Sounds other than music can be relaxing and healing. Many people enjoy listening to records of tuneful birdsong or the rhythmic rumble of breakers on the shore. Several recordings, available on cassette or compact disc, blend the sounds of nature with music. For instance, a recording called "Southwest Suite" features various animal sounds ranging from the mountain chickadee to the canyon frog, along with soothing instrumental music, while "The Complete Sounds of Tranquility" blends the sounds of the ocean with well-known melodies such as Beethoven's "Moonlight Sonata."

There are also recordings of the sounds of nature that do not include music, so people who don't enjoy music would probably greatly enjoy these.

Gardening for Pleasure

As all gardeners know, great pleasure can come from turning over the earth by hand or with a tool, planting seeds or seedlings and watching flowers or vegetables thrive and grow. Indeed, horticultural therapy was used during World War II to help members of the armed forces recover from shock. Today, many retirement and nursing homes have gardens for therapeutic purposes.

One such is Westside Care Centre, a long-term care facility in Westbank in British Columbia's Okanagan Valley. Both residents and people in the day program called Elderwell work in the series of raised beds just outside the building. Beds, containing a mix of flowering plants and vegetables, are raised to make it easier for elders, some of whom are in wheelchairs, to work in them without stooping, and their positioning means that residents who aren't well enough to participate and must remain indoors can see the activity through the windows and derive enjoyment from the plantings.

Sue Yerex, a nurse at Westside, describes herself as the gardening facilitator, pointing out that the elders do almost all the work. She tells a heartwarming story of two participants in the Elderwell program.

Both are male, and both have some dementia. One is a former businessman and initially insisted he didn't want to get his hands dirty gardening. The other is a former pest control officer who enjoys gardening. Yerex persuaded the former businessman to at least give gardening a try and began to show him what he had to do. Then the former pest control officer took over the teaching role. The learner now derives huge pleasure from gardening, saying, "Oh, wonderful! Oh, look how big they are growing!" And the teacher has derived a great sense of self-worth out of being useful and having something to give.

"Gardening helped to build the friendship between the two," Yerex says. As well as working together in the Elderwell program, they meet and go for walks together now. "They really care about each other," Yerex says. "If one fellow doesn't come, the other asks us, 'Well, did you phone and find out if he is okay?'"

She is happy with the gardening program and the fact that it gives people an activity they enjoy, as well as giving them a sense of achievement. "I think it is really successful therapy," she says, "and I would recommend it to others." Even people who are quite incapacitated can get involved, she points out. For instance, someone who is bedridden could put plants in window boxes or tend houseplants using an over-the-bed table on wheels.

Remembering When

Reminiscence therapy has not yet officially arrived in Canada at time of writing. But it is, in fact, probably practised by a good many psychiatrists and psychologists when they are working with elderly patients.

One such is Dr. Pearl Karal, a psychologist practising in Toronto.

Reminiscence therapy, Dr. Karal explains, simply means encouraging elders to think back and recall happy events in their earlier lives. "This brings back a lot of positive elements that they have forgotten. It helps them balance the negative qualities present in their current life.

"You use triggers to bring out memories if this is necessary. One trigger might be: do you remember anything that made you extremely happy when you were 20? Or describe your 21st birthday. You search around for positives until you find some sort of spark. Then you lead them back, using gentle questions.

"One of the things I recommend caregivers do is get their care receivers to tell them about their childhood, what their schooling was like, what kind of clothes they wore, what type of playthings they had, what kind of friendships. For one thing, this helps the caregiver understand the older person. It also gives the older person something to offer the caregiver other than complaints and criticisms. And it provides a bond because the caregiver now knows more about the older person."

Dr. Karal, who points out that music therapy is often a form of reminiscence therapy, often finds that elders' long-term memories are excellent. "Often they bring out all sorts of details that they themselves had forgotten, and they are fascinated by what they discover."

Photographs of happy occasions throughout your care receiver's life, starting in childhood, are effective keys to unlock memories. If they are not already in albums, creating and annotating albums will be an enjoyable pastime for you both.

As well as probing for happy memories, you might also help an elder think back to times when he or she achieved signal success of some kind. Comments and questions such as "I understand you were a champion long-distance swimmer. Tell me about it," or "What was the biggest number of sales you ever made in one week?" will make this elder feel proud of past successes, and hence happy.

If, as a caregiver, you can gently encourage an elder to open the box of memories at a time when she or he is cranky and perhaps experiencing some pain, this is especially valuable. The elder will cease to be preoccupied with problems or discomfort and will enjoy the human interaction that takes place as you display a keen interest in the memories that are being shared with you.

Massage Therapy, Shiatsu and Reflexology

All these practices involve touching and may therefore be of help to care receivers both physically and psychologically, since they may lack—and crave—physical contact of some kind, especially if they are widowed.

In all three cases, you should make sure any practitioner your care receiver consults is fully qualified and has good credentials. To start a search, you might ask around among friends and acquaintances for referrals.

Massage, or Swedish massage as it is sometimes called, has been a popular form of therapy for many thousands of years. Properly done, massage can stimulate the circulation, respiration and glandular activity and secretions, as well as relaxing tense muscles and generally reducing stress.

The only provinces regulating massage at time of writing are Ontario and British Columbia. In these provinces, masseurs must take specified training courses before being licensed as registered massage therapists. Those who have done so are entitled to use the acronym RMT after their names—something to look for if you or your care receiver feel like some invigorating therapy.

Shiatsu and reflexology also date back thousands of years and are based on oriental beliefs and practices. Shiatsu practitioners apply pressure, usually with fingers or thumbs, to certain points on the body's surface, in the belief that this stimulates a flow of energy by releasing any blockages to the energy flow. It has proven to be of help in treating arthritic and sciatic discomfort, neck and back pain, muscle tension, headaches, stiffness and fatigue.

Shiatsu therapists are not yet licensed in Canada. Timothy Phillips, a Toronto shiatsu therapist who is a member of the board of directors of the Shiatsu Therapy Association of Ontario, describes the training he and his peers must take. "Someone who is a member of our association has done a 2,200-hour program of both western sciences and eastern—a lot of pathology, physiology, anatomy, clinical science and practice." As with massage therapists, you or your care receiver should patronize only therapists who have been fully trained and have diplomas or certificates to show for it. As Phillips says, "Someone could ostensibly do a weekend course and put out a shingle as a shiatsu practitioner. And that could be dangerous."

Some shiatsu therapists specialize in treating older people, Phillips says. And some will make house calls.

Reflexology is based on the belief that specific points on the soles of the feet correspond to specific parts of the body, including organs and glands. Stimulation of these points through pressure and massage is believed to improve the condition and function of the corresponding body part, not least by improving the blood circulation to that part. Reflexologists, some of whom work on the hands as well as the feet, treat headaches, backaches, poor circulation and general stress, among other ailments. They claim that the technique is well suited to the generalized stress and stiffness experienced by older people. "It is good for the older person," says reflexologist Lynda Fiset who works at Toronto's Aesthetic Health Clinic. "It helps the body's natural healing process. Anyone who has regular reflexology sessions will have improved health. Elderly people really enjoy it."

Reflexology is another unregulated therapy. To be sure you and your care receiver are dealing with a fully trained therapist who maintains high standards of practice, look for one who is a member of the Reflexology Association of Canada.

Aromatherapy

"Most of my clients are seniors. And, yes, they seem to benefit from this. I always do a follow-up next day, and they always report feeling better, sleeping well and feeling more relaxed and comfortable."

The speaker is Jody Rathaur, an aroma massage therapist living and working in Oshawa, Ontario. Like some other aroma massage therapists, Rathaur makes house calls. She has a brief advance telephone consultation with new clients so that she knows what conditions she will be treating. Then she massages them for one hour, using whatever aromatic oils are appropriate.

"Their prominent problems are arthritis, general pain, poor circulation and a lot of anxiety," she says.

Rathaur is administering a therapy that both ancient Greeks and ancient Romans are known to have practised. It uses the healing powers its proponents believe are associated with certain fragrances.

The essential oils used in aromatherapy may be administered in one of four ways. You may be massaged using them, as are Rathaur's clients. You may inhale their fragrances. You may add them to water you bathe in. Or, far less commonly, you may ingest them.

If you choose to inhale the fragrance of aromatherapy's oils, put a few drops on a light bulb or a vacuum cleaner's filter, your pillowslip or your humidifier.

Some commonly reported effects of specific fragrances are as follows: rosemary stimulates, lavender calms, chamomile and eucalyptus relieve headaches, neroli (derived from oranges) is a relaxant, jasmine may help depressed people feel more energetic and basil relieves anxiety and nervous spasms.

Bridget LeChat, who teaches at the Canadian National School of Aromatherapy in Mississauga, Ontario, originally came from South Africa. There, she says, knowledge about and the practice of aromatherapy is far more advanced than in Canada. Back home, she says, aromatherapy has proven to be really beneficial to elders. "Every time someone goes home, I ask them to bring back certain oils that are easily obtainable in drug stores there.

"While aromatherapy works on the nervous system," she continues, "it is designed to bring harmony to the person's body. And when you align the mind, body and spirit into one, that person feels better about himself or herself.

"You know, a lot of older people like the smell of lavender. So if you want to create a feeling of well-being, just use plain lavender in a mild solution as an infusion."

However, neither you nor your care receiver should dash out to a health food store to buy aromatic oils to treat a specific medical condition without first consulting a qualified aromatherapist. And be aware, LeChat says, that a considerable number of conditions should not be treated with aromatherapy. People with chronic asthma, those who have just had surgery, people with a tendency to epilepsy, those with advanced cancer and those with severe skin conditions should not use aromatherapy. LeChat also never recommends the ingestion of aromatic oils, which can induce headaches and nausea in some people, and some of which are toxic if swallowed.

In addition, Jody Rathaur counsels, some aromatic oils lower blood pressure, so they should never be used by people who already have a blood pressure level below normal.

When looking for a good aromatherapist, you should first ascertain where and for how long this person trained, and ask for evidence of certification. There are several schools in this country that teach aromatherapy. In addition to LeChat's, for instance, there is also the Canadian School of Aromatherapy in Toronto. Membership in the Canadian Federation of Aromatherapists is also a plus. And, LeChat counsels, "Ask how long they have been in the business. In aromatherapy, proficiency comes with experience."

Humor Therapy

Dr. Bob Hatfield, who works at Calgary's Foothills Hospital, is one of many people who believe in the curative power of laughter and humor. He tells the story of one patient, which certainly appears to bear out his belief.

The woman was in her early 70s and had been brought in as being in need of emergency care due to heart failure. Indeed, surgery showed that she did indeed have heart problems. But it also showed that she had cancer of the right lung, which had spread to other areas and was too advanced to be treatable. Indeed, Dr. Hatfield believed she probably would not live more than a few weeks. He broke the news to her as gently as possible, then asked if she fully understood what he had said. "She said, 'Yes. I've got cancer and I'm not going to live very long,'" he recalls. "There was a pause, then she suddenly said, 'Can I tell you a joke?' I was startled, but I said, 'Okay, but one rule. If you tell me a joke, I tell you a joke.'" Which is exactly what happened. Clearly, this patient shared Dr. Hatfield's belief in and use of humor.

Within a day or so, she began asking when she could go home, since her husband, who was in his 80s, needed looking after. Believing she would never go home again, Dr. Hatfield said he would do what he could. In fact, a week later he arranged for a transfer to a hospital in her home town, saying the trip would tire her too much for her to go straight home.

About four months later, he was speaking to the woman's physician about another patient, and happened to ask how long the woman had lived. "Oh," the physician said, "She's at home. She stayed in the hospital a few days but she said she had to go home."

About eight months after that, the woman's daughter called Dr. Hatfield and asked if he would see her mother, who was still very much alive but failing. "Under my breath I said: if she is still alive she has passed with flying colors." Hatfield says. He readily agreed to see her, and discovered that by now both lungs were full of cancer, as was her chest wall. As before, they exchanged jokes. Every time after that when they saw each other, they always exchanged jokes.

Instead of a few short weeks, this patient lived for another 18 months.

"There was no question," Dr. Hatfield says. "Her deliberate use of humor, of providing a laugh for others and allowing people like me to try to provide one for her, and her fierce determination and her faith that she could do it—all these combined to extend this woman's life far beyond what it should have been. She was just a great inspiration."

She was also fortunate in encountering Dr. Hatfield. If she had instead encountered someone who said, "How can you joke when you know you're dying?" she probably would have stopped telling jokes and died much sooner.

Thanks to Dr. Hatfield, Foothills Hospital is one of many health care centres that have humor rooms or humor carts, which volunteers take from ward to ward so patients can borrow humorous books and magazines or audiotapes or videotapes. As well, they may stock items such as clown noses, face paints, squirt guns, games and toys. Queen Elizabeth Hospital in Toronto has a Laughter Lounge. Humber Memorial Hospital in Weston, Ontario, has a humor cart. Grand River Hospital, which serves the Kitchener-Waterloo area in Ontario, has Joke Junction, a humor room, and also humor carts.

Dr. Ken Shonk, Joke Junction's founder, says hospitals in Guelph and Stratford now practise humor therapy, and Joan Ginn, the volunteer coordinator of the Grand River program, says health care centres right across Ontario and beyond have been calling in asking about the program.

One of the first people to write extensively about the benefits of laughter was Norman Cousins, who had a disease doctors said would kill him, and who used laughter as therapy to help him to a complete recovery. (He died many years later of unrelated causes.) In his book, *Anatomy of an Illness as Perceived by the Patient: Reflections on Healing and Regeneration*, he details some of the beneficial effects of laughter. It exercises the lungs and the diaphragm. Associated as it is with deeper respiration, it causes an increase in the uptake of oxygen. It helps in the control of pain, not least because it causes the body to produce more endorphins, which are natural painkillers. As well as endorphins, it causes the brain to produce more catecholamines, which have been shown to reduce inflammation.

In addition, laughter can reduce or even eliminate tensions in the upper body—the neck, shoulders, chest and abdomen. It lowers blood pressure and pulse rate. Initial research also appears to show that laughter can give a boost to the body's immune system by increasing its production of immunoglobin, a substance that fights off viruses.

It can also improve mood and relationships. At Grand River Hospital, Dr. Shonk says, "We are not curing cancer with this: what we are doing is helping people take control of their lives, improving the quality of life. I see people who use humor when they're sick and draw people to them, instead of people who bitch and complain about every little thing and drive people away from them."

Dr. Shonk also finds that, once patients have used humor as a method of relaxing, they find it far easier to communicate with those caring for them and to discuss serious matters such as their chances of survival. "This is very, very valuable," he says.

Joan Ginn, Grand River's coordinator, says older men greatly enjoy watching funny videos they enjoyed when they were young—Abbott and Costello, perhaps, or the Three Stooges. Elderly women really like watching *Driving Miss Daisy*, she finds.

Ginn believes profoundly in humor therapy. She speaks of one man who had had a stroke and who made no response whatever, either by voice or facial expression, when approached. When fitted with earphones and given a tape player with a funny audiocassette, he beamed. As well, she points out, quite a few patients come back to the hospital after they have been discharged and offer to make a donation to the program—a video perhaps or a book—which is a clear indication that they found the program beneficial.

Jackie Rodger is a patient of Dr. Shonk's. She was married for nearly 30 years to John, who broke his neck when he was 19 and from then on was unable to move the lower half of his body. For all that, he became a successful insurance underwriting consultant. An award named after him is made annually for professionalism, integrity, leadership and the pursuit of excellence.

"John used humor," Jackie remembers. "If you ask the people who knew him, he is probably as well remembered for his sense of humor as he is for any of those attributes. Humor was just part of his daily life. He used it all the time. It was part of his coping mechanism." In consequence, humor became part of her life too, and when John died four years ago at the age of 61, she fell back on humor as part of her own coping mechanism, watching a comedy video or a sitcom when she felt down.

The beauty of humor therapy, of course, is that it is so readily available. Libraries are rich sources of humorous books, magazines and videos. Join your care receiver in a great physical workout by watching *A Fish Called Wanda* or a Fawlty Towers video. Read *Forrest Gump* or an Edwin Newman book. As Jackie Rodger says, "Everybody should start bringing humor into their lives. Not just people taking care of people—everybody should do it."

Color Therapy

Here's a word you probably have not met before: chromotherapy. It means healing by the use of colors, and it is very much on the cutting edge of therapies. Physicians who practise chromotherapy most often shine colored lights on the sites on the body that require healing. As well, however—and this is how laypeople like you and me can practise chromotherapy—the colors of furnishings, clothing worn and other objects in the immediate environment can have an effect on a person's mood and general health.

For instance, a vivid sky blue is believed by chromotherapists to be the most tranquilizing color in the spectrum. When engineers construct bridges high above water or chasms, they sometimes paint them blue to help calm potential suicides, who might otherwise jump. If your care receiver looks for a while at an object this color, she or he will probably experience a feeling of calmness, a slower pulse rate and a lower body temperature, among other things, due to changes in the brain's secretion of hormones.

By contrast, red is believed to cause excitement. Anyone exposed to red can experience increased blood pressure. He or she will likely also breathe faster. Clearly, you could be making a big mistake if you furnish a bedroom with red fabrics.

And, yes, red can increase the appetite. That quite a few restaurants feature red or red-and-white checked table linen is no accident.

If buying new bedroom furnishings for your care receiver, consider green fabrics. Green is considered to be a cooling and soothing color. It can have a calming effect, both physically and mentally. It can also relieve tension and produce a sense of warmth.

In search of a contrasting hue for the bedroom? Try brown. Chromotherapists say brown surroundings are good to work, play and sleep in, since brown can help reduce irritability and promote physical and mental health.

Chromotherapists find yellow to be a digestive aid. A dash of yellow—the color of sunlight—in a room is a cheerful note. However, the presence of a mass of yellows may be stressful and may cause people to become angry.

Also avoid mauve, which is believed to have a highly depressing effect.

As with music therapy, however, the likes and dislikes of the recipient should prevail. No matter that green seems to have a soothing effect: if your care receiver, like many people, detests green, don't include it in the color scheme.

CHAPTER SEVEN

Opening Up the Lines of Communication

If you are to be an effective caregiver, you must be able to communicate well with your care receiver in order to find out, among other things, which behaviors of yours are pleasing and welcome and which are not. But sometimes, over the years of living apart and seeing little of one another, a caregiver and her care receiver parent may have drifted and may no longer communicate well. Equally, someone giving care to a partner or peer may find communication difficult because the care receiver has problems—deafness, perhaps, or dementia.

In this chapter, we'll look at opening up the lines of communication and, in so doing, starting to build or rebuild good relationships.

Good Conversational Settings and Habits

Communication is easier when you are both at the same level. Never hold a conversation with someone who is sitting in a chair or lying in bed while you stand towering over this person. Also make sure there is little background noise, with no loud or distracting sounds.

When your care receiver is talking to you, lean forward slightly and maintain eye contact. Both indicate that you are listening carefully. If you gaze around the room or out of the window, this person will assume one of two things: you aren't listening, or you are bored stiff.

People tend to speak in a higher tone of voice when they are upset, in a lower tone when they are calm. As well, lower tones are easier for people with a hearing deficit to hear. So use a low tone of voice when conversing with your care receiver.

Older people often speak slowly. If your care receiver has just finished a sentence, don't jump in with a reply right away. "Many elderly people have sensory losses," says Ginny Schedewitz, a regional manager in London, Ontario, with Comcare (Canada), a large home health care agency. "Their hearing or visual acuity has decreased. It is important to give them time to finish a thought or to collect their thoughts during a conversation."

By the same token, if you sense an unfinished thought or train of reasoning, say something like, "That's really interesting, Uncle James. Can you tell me more about it?"

If the topic you are discussing requires you both to express an opinion, unless your care receiver requires some kind of stimulus, ask this person to state an opinion first before you jump in with your ideas.

Try to make statements as uncritical as possible. For instance, rather than saying "I'm constantly furious at you because you leave water all over the bathroom floor and the towels in a heap on the chair," try, "You know, if you tidied up after yourself when you use the bathroom, I'd be a whole lot happier, and I'd have more time to do things with you."

Give praise where praise is deserved, and look on the positive side wherever possible. For instance, if this person can dress but can't manage shoelaces, and says, "Dammit, I can't do these laces up," say, "Yes, but you dressed yourself entirely. You even tied your tie. That's great. Why don't we buy some slip-ons so you can do the entire job?" But make sure your statements are sincere: don't be patronizing.

If your care receiver's opinion differs from your own, respect her or his right to hold that opinion. Listen carefully and don't become excited or annoyed. Say something like "You know, I beg to differ. I may be wrong, but here's how I see it." Do not say, "You're quite wrong. That's not the way it is."

If you ask your care receiver how he or she is feeling today, and the response is, "Rather low, I'm afraid," Schedewitz says, "Don't offer suggestions as to how to cheer up. Instead, explore with this person the reasons for feeling low. Sometimes, if an elder is given the opportunity to ventilate the low feeling, this may resolve a low mood." For this to happen, you must validate the elder's mood by saying feeling low is a perfectly normal consequence of starting to lose your sight— or whatever reason the elder gave you.

Bad Conversational Habits

Don't interrupt your care receiver unless you need to have something explained or made clear. Hear this person out, even if you disagree strongly with the views being expressed. If you feel you should express your opinion, wait until he or she has finished talking, then politely do so.

Some people tend to "talk down" to elders—as if, perhaps, they believe them to be entering second childhood. For the majority of elders, there is no such thing as a second childhood. Unless your care receiver is cognitively impaired, behave as you would if you were talking to any adult.

If you don't quite understand what an elder is saying, don't just move on to something else. Ask for clarification, or you may miss something important.

Never finish a sentence for your care receiver. She or he may be searching for the appropriate words or names, and should be permitted to complete that search. Of course, if this person stops in the middle of a sentence and says, "Drat, what was that woman's name?" you should help out.

The Right Kinds of Questions

Ask open-ended questions (unless this person is cognitively impaired). Ask, "How are you feeling today?" which could be the start of a whole conversation. "Are you feeling well today?" may elicit a one-word answer which signals the end of this particular conversation. Never ask "How are we today?" which is demeaning. And ask one question at a time to avoid confusion.

Ask an elder what things were like in times you can't remember or never knew. Maybe this person recalls seeing a jet aircraft for the first time, and can talk about people's reactions to it and to having flown in it. He or she will enjoy the recollecting, and you'll broaden your own horizons and gather new knowledge. Also, Schedewitz points out, you can start a conversation by asking a question about something in the elder's vicinity. "That needle case is pretty. And it's handmade! Who made it for you, and when?" may start a flow of recollections.

Ask questions you know your care receiver will enjoy answering. Most people like talking about themselves and their past accomplishments. So go ahead, ask how well this person remembers being nominated citizen of the year or winning a prize for photography.

Doctors and hospital staff routinely call patients by their first names these days, no matter what their age or their wishes. Perhaps they feel this will put patients at ease. But, as Schedewitz points out, "Many seniors are offended by this type of familiarity. They should be treated with more respect." So if someone new comes into the house, ask your care receiver, "Would you like this person to call you Mrs. Simmonds or Marian?"

Older people sometimes use generalizations to reveal feelings they have. For instance, your care receiver may say, "Doesn't everyone hate going to the dentist?" Don't answer, "Probably." Instead, say something like, "Sounds as though you hate going to the dentist." You'll probably receive an affirmative reply, and you can then go on to find out whether this person dislikes all dentists or just Dr. McCavity, and whether he or she hasn't seen a dentist in years and hence doesn't know that dentistry is now relatively painless.

Ask, rather than tell. Don't say, "Please get out of bed and walk up and down the corridor so you get some exercise and I can make your bed." Instead, say, "How would you like to get up and walk up and down the corridor? You'll feel better for the exercise and I'll be able to make your bed."

Appropriate Topics of Conversation

Talk about some of the funny things that happened to one or both of you in the past. Laughter is a great lifter of the spirits and great exercise for the lungs.

Reminisce about your shared past. Reminiscences of good times are happy and healing. You might use props—photograph albums are good props, and collections of stamps or coins may be helpful too.

Remember that people love hearing stories about themselves. Talk to your care receiver about her or his past life and successes. You'll give great enjoyment in so doing, and may open a magic box of memories in return.

Elders like to reminisce, but they should also be encouraged to think about the present and the future. "Use their past experiences in a positive way to demonstrate to them how they can effectively cope in the present and how they can utilize their experiences to cope in the future," Schedewitz says. For instance, if a care receiver was a manager or a secretary or part of a team during the career years, this person has much to offer seniors' or volunteer groups and should be encouraged to join. Those who were always good cooks should be encouraged to produce goods for bake sales or to cook meals often for family and friends.

Never make a promise you may not be able to keep. "Promise you won't ever put me in a home," should be met with something like, "You know I'll do everything I possibly can to keep you out of permanent care." If your care receiver persists and says, "No, I want you to promise," say, "Look, I'll do everything I can, as I said. But not knowing what the future holds, I can't promise. You wouldn't want me to make a promise I might be forced to break, would you?"

If an elder wants to talk about her or his demise, don't change the subject or say, "Come on, Dad, you don't want to talk about that. You've years of life in you." He *does* want to talk about that, so ask him questions. Perhaps ask whether he would want a funeral and, if so, what favorite hymns he would want to have sung. If he starts to talk about dying at an inappropriate time—perhaps when visitors are present—tell him you'll discuss it with him later when you can give your full attention to the subject.

Just as young people should have goals, so should elders. If you listen carefully to an elder reminiscing, you will probably gain some insight about what might be appropriate goals. For instance, if this person mourns friends who have died, you might encourage him or her into achieving a short-term goal—writing a letter to or visiting with a friend who is still here. Then introduce topics of conversation that will encourage this person to think farther ahead. In winter, ask what plantings she or he plans to buy next spring when the gardening season opens. At the end of a vacation, ask whether a similar vacation would be enjoyable a year from now, or whether this person has plans for something different or more ambitious.

Nonverbal Communication

Learn to be a good listener. This means watching your care receiver's facial expressions and body language, as well as listening carefully to what is being said. The eyes are particularly expressive. Also listen to the tone of voice this person is using.

Unless you know your care receiver does not like to be touched, use a squeeze of the hand or a tap on the back of the hand or the arm to emphasize a point. Say goodbye or goodnight with a hug or an arm around the shoulders. Use touch as a lubricant to conversation.

Watch to make sure you're not overloading your care receiver with information. The signs of overload are likely to be agitation and confusion.

Smile whenever a smile is appropriate. Smiles are friendly—and infectious.

Here are some nonverbal clues to a person's state of mind or attitude that you should be aware of and watch for while conversing with your care receiver:

- Folding the arms across the chest is a sign that this person feels defensive.
- Standing with arms akimbo—hands on hips, elbows out and away from the body—is a signal to keep away from this person.
- Biting the bottom lip is usually a sign of anger.
- Dilation of the pupils of the eyes indicates that this person is enjoying something seen or experienced.

- A fixed stare, with the eyes open wide, indicates that this person is threatening you.

During her many years of working with elders, Schedewitz has noticed that if you ask them how they are coping at home, if in fact they are not coping well, they will probably look away from you while claiming that they are indeed coping.

In general, if a person responds to your question but does not look at you, you are probably not being told the truth. "I'm fine," said while staring out of the window is an indication that this person probably is far from fine.

Likewise, if your care receiver says, "No, I'm not in pain at all," but frowns or grimaces when moving, you are probably not being told the truth.

How to Draw Out Someone Who Doesn't Want to Talk

If your care receiver has suddenly become cantankerous and silent, consider taking the following steps.

First, make sure you approach this person in a warm and positive way. Say that you empathize with whatever is being felt. When this person does say anything, listen carefully to everything that is said, not just to those remarks that indicate bad temper: you are looking for clues about what caused this mood.

Ask this person if the mood is one of anger and, if it is, encourage ventilation of this anger. If the reason for the anger has any validity, say so.

Never take negative behavior personally. Almost certainly, this person is angry not at you but at some limitation or loss recently experienced.

You may also hit a snag if your care receiver is about to receive a new form of therapy or undergo surgery. You want to discuss the therapy or surgery with this person, but you may be told, "I don't want to talk about it." You have a choice of responses to this.

You could ask whether it would be more appropriate to discuss the therapy or surgery at a later date.

You could provide this person with written material or videos that describe the therapy or surgery.

You could announce your availability to discuss the subject at any time in the future when you are asked.

You could suggest that this person discuss the subject with a physician or therapist, or perhaps with someone who has experienced this type of therapy or surgery.

However, don't ever force your care receiver to talk about a subject if she or he really doesn't want to. If this person says flatly, "I will not talk about this with you," by all means try one of the approaches listed above, or ask if this person would be willing to talk to someone else about this subject, but under no circumstances insist, "No, you will talk about it now and with me."

Healing Bad Relationships

If you and your care receiver have some unfinished business that is causing bad feelings between you, use the following procedure in order to get the matter out into the open and settled once and for all.

First, the cause of the bad feelings should be expressed and thoroughly explored. Then you should discuss methods that were used in the past to handle a bad situation, and utilize them in order to resolve the problem that is currently affecting the relationship.

Here's an example. When your mother first came to live with you, she wanted to have supper at five-thirty because she retires early. You had always served supper at seven-thirty. You checked with other family members. Yes, six-thirty was fine by them. And by your mother.

Today the unfinished business is your mother's habit of always wanting to know where you are going, who—if anyone—you are going to meet, what you are going to be doing. When you return, she asks the same questions, until you feel like a child who can't be trusted out of her sight. Because of this, you have stopped telling her where you are going and what you are going to be doing. When she questions you, you simply don't reply.

So now you remind your mother how readily she accepted the compromise solution over the supper hour. Suggest a compromise would be in order now. If she doesn't ask all those questions, you will tell her why you're going out, and when you return home you'll tell her briefly how you got on and whether anything unusual or interesting happened while you were out. Chances are, your mother will accept this compromise solution.

Or maybe your care receiver starts criticizing a third person—perhaps a secondary caregiver. For example, your sister Susan takes your mother out shopping every Friday morning. "She rushes me off my feet," your mother complains. "I don't enjoy going shopping any more." Question your mother closely so that you understand her feelings and she has a chance to ventilate them. Yes, she is rushed in every store. Yes, when they stop for coffee, Susan wants to leave long before she does.

The solution here is a three-way nonconfrontational conversation. If you referee it skilfully, ensuring both participants remain calm and reasonable, Susan will finally realize that the Friday morning outing is the high point of her mother's week. It is the one time she is out and about in the community, and her one chance to look at new products and new fashions in the stores, and—while drinking coffee—to people-watch, a favorite occupation of hers. For her part, your mother will realize that her habit of reading all the ingredients on the labels of three products before making a choice is irritating, as is her practice of minutely examining racks of clothing she has no intention of buying. And 50 minutes over one cup of coffee is a trifle long.

Now, both your mother and Susan understand each other better. Both compromise a little, and no more criticisms are heard.

In general then, as you have seen, communicating effectively with your care receiver calls for some special techniques and skills. But overall, use of the qualities of empathy, warmth, tact, calmness and nonjudgmental objectivity will do much to ensure that your conversations are enjoyable and instructive experiences for you both.

CHAPTER EIGHT

Coping With Common Physical Conditions

Alma Battersby's husband Ken, 62, has had Parkinsons for more than seven years. As well as the usual common symptoms—notably tremoring hands—he also experiences confusion and disturbed sleep, which are side effects of the medication he takes.

As well as general caregiving practices, Alma has found she has had to modify her behavior and habits because of the changes in Ken brought on by Parkinsons. For instance, she used to enjoy playing cards with Ken and friends who also live in White Rock, B.C., but, because his shaking hands embarrass him, he no longer plays cards. "We are both very social people," Alma says. "We are still accepted socially as before, but sometimes he feels really shaky and doesn't want to go out."

Many jobs Ken tackles turn into clutter because of his confusion, which has affected his organizational skills. Alma finds this annoys her, but tries to contain her annoyance. "And the sleep disturbance is a really big factor," she says. "He is up and down and up and down all night, rattling pills and doing all kinds of things that just drive me bananas. I don't get my sleep and become cranky. I have sought some guidance and I belong to a support group, so I'm working on trying to correct this situation."

If, like Alma, you are a caregiver to someone who has a specific condition, be it Parkinsons or diabetes or hypertension or any other physical disability associated with aging, you will probably have to make an extra effort, over and above the normal duties involved in caregiving, to help your care receiver and to cope with his or her problems.

This chapter will explore just what those extra duties may be in the case of 11 common conditions associated with aging.

Arthritis

Both osteoarthritis and rheumatoid arthritis affect the joints and cause mild to severe discomfort.

For all that, people with arthritis should not give up movement and exercise. The family physician or a physiotherapist may have pre-scribed a certain course of exercise; your role is to ensure that your care receiver follows that course regularly. Ask the physician about weightlifting; some research has shown that people with osteoarthritis experience decreased discomfort and increased mobility after strength training.

You should also be aware of a number of household aids that people with arthritic hands may find helpful: a heavy-duty nonslip elastic "sleeve" to slip over a doorknob, a cutting board with spikes to hold food steady, specially shaped cutlery for hands that find it hard to grip, for instance.

If arthritis makes general movement and getting up difficult, grab bars in places such as a shower stall and alongside a toilet may be your best solution. In Chapter Ten you'll find descriptions of some other assistive devices that may be helpful to someone who has arthritis.

Diabetes

Diabetes is a disease in which working cells associated with insulin throughout the body are unable to use food energy properly. If diabetes is left untreated and high blood sugar levels continue, serious complications such as heart attack, stroke, blindness and kidney disease can occur.

There are two main types of diabetes: Type I, insulin-dependent diabetes, and Type II, noninsulin-dependent diabetes. Type I diabetes usually occurs in people under 40 years of age and requires a routine of insulin injections, meal planning and activity. Type II diabetes usually occurs in people over 40 years of age and may be treated with meal planning alone, meal planning and pills, or meal planning and insulin injections.

If your care receiver has diabetes, you must make sure this person follows the diet prescribed in every detail, and adheres to the recommended exercise regimen. Making sure the correct dosages of any medications used are taken at prescribed times is also extremely important.

Find out from the family physician when and how often to check the level of blood sugar, and also ensure a record is kept of the readings and shown to the physician.

If your care receiver is diabetic, you should be aware of several risk factors:

- obesity—help your care receiver not to become overweight
- smoking—try to help this person to quit
- physical and emotional stress—try to ensure your care receiver is not stressed

Diabetes can damage the circulation in the feet, causing them to lose sensation. You or your care receiver should inspect, wash and dry them daily. If minor breaks in the skin of the feet appear and do not heal swiftly, consult the family physician right away. If corns or calluses appear, do not treat them yourself; instead, consult a podiatrist.

Diabetes can cause vision problems, so encourage your care receiver to have regular checkups by an ophthalmologist.

Emphysema and Chronic Bronchitis

Both these diseases cause obstructions in the lungs, often making breathing difficult and causing the patient to inhale insufficient oxygen. Their collective name is chronic obstructive pulmonary disease, or COPD.

Make sure your care receiver takes medications as directed, and has an inhaled bronchodilator on hand to use in emergencies. (Bronchodilators relax the muscles around the airways, making breathing easier.)

You or your care receiver should ask the family physician—or perhaps a physiotherapist—to recommend a set of exercises for the patient, and make sure this exercise regime is followed. If the recommended exercise is walking, in winter this might be done in a local mall so the patient is inhaling warm air.

Breathing exercises should also be prescribed. Again, make sure they are done regularly.

If your care receiver still smokes, do everything in your power to persuade her or him to quit. If you are unsuccessful, ask the family physician to try. Many elderly people have great respect for those in white coats, and the physician may be able to persuade this person to have a trial period using a nicotine patch. As well, environments where there is second-hand smoke should be avoided.

Some people with COPD are susceptible to certain substances, among them perfume and fumes from paints and household sprays. If this is true of your care receiver, make sure exposure to these substances is avoided. Dust may also be an irritant; if so, vacuum often and thoroughly, and dust with a damp cloth (it will pick up the dust rather than scattering it).

The family physician will probably recommend vaccination against influenza and also against pneumococcal pneumonia. If so, make sure your care receiver has these shots.

Counsel your care receiver to eat slowly. Eating slowly helps conserve the body's supply of oxygen and so reduces breathlessness. If convenient, she or he might try eating six small meals rather than three big ones every day, in order to lower the body's oxygen need during digestion.

Hearing Loss

Many older people experience some hearing loss, with sharp sounds (most consonants) and high ones going long before vowel sounds and low ones are lost.

The most important task for you is to learn how to speak to your care receiver so that you are heard more clearly.

First, ensure that you are close together and that there is plenty of light on your face so he or she can see your mouth move and the expression on your face. Deaf people can read quite a lot from lip movements and facial expressions, even if they are not accomplished lip readers. Also make sure you sit or stand directly in front of this person, and if he or she has a "good" ear speak to that side.

If your care receiver normally wears glasses and/or a hearing aid, make sure they are worn during a conversation. Also make sure there is little or no background noise, and speak in a clear, distinct voice, perhaps a little more slowly than usual. But do not shout or exaggerate mouth movements, and do not chew gum or smoke while you are talking.

There are a number of useful signalling devices for use by those with impaired hearing—telephones with lights that flash when they ring, and lights that come on when a doorbell rings, among others. The family physician can probably refer you to a centre or centres dealing in such devices.

Heart Disease

Aging hearts are subject to a number of conditions. These include atherosclerosis, which causes narrowing of the arteries by building up fatty deposits on their walls; congestive heart failure, which occurs when the heart pumps less efficiently and blood pools in the tissues causing congestion; and heart attack, which happens when the blood supply to part of the heart muscle is cut off and that part starts to die.

Heart patients quite commonly experience angina pectoris, a pain in the chest experienced when a part of the heart muscle is receiving an insufficient supply of blood. In order to avoid angina attacks, you should help your care receiver to avoid excessive physical activity and any emotional stress or upset.

If your care receiver has had a heart attack, ask the family physician how soon certain activities can be resumed. There is no set norm here; the answer will be predicated on the patient's rate of healing and the extent of the damage to the heart.

Almost everyone who has a heart attack is scared and temporarily depressed. If depression becomes serious, however, this person needs help. If your care receiver exhibits any of the following signs, a visit to the family physician is in order: persistent loss of appetite, sleeping too little or too much, thoughts of suicide or death, trouble concentrating, loss of interest in former pursuits and hobbies, personal slovenliness.

If your care receiver has been a really hearty eater in the past, now is a good time to encourage her or him to cut back. Heavy eaters place a large strain on their hearts, and people with heart disease should keep their weight normal or even slightly below normal.

Hypertension

Hypertension means consistently high blood pressure. Most people who have it do not know until a physician, using an instrument called a sphygmomanometer, takes a reading and finds it to be high.

If your care receiver has been given medication for hypertension, ensure that this is taken as prescribed on an ongoing basis. Medication controls but does not cure high blood pressure, so if it is discontinued pressure will rise again. If this person is overweight, suggest an altered and healthier diet and plenty of exercise in an effort to get weight down. Losing weight almost always results in lower blood pressure, and exercise is great at fighting stress, which can also cause high blood pressure.

If this person is indeed under stress, try to find other ways to promote relaxation, such as playing with a pet, listening to music together or going for a stroll somewhere in the country or in a park.

A high salt intake, smoking and caffeine are all capable of causing high blood pressure. So try to ensure your care receiver restricts the use of salt, try to help him or her to quit smoking and try to limit caffeine drinks to no more than four a day.

Incontinence

Inability to prevent a flow of urine is far more common than you may think: estimates show that at one time or another as many as six people in 10 will suffer from it. Your main task is to convince your care receiver not to be ashamed of this disability. Perhaps this statistic will help; one often feels less ashamed if one realizes one is far from alone.

Your next task is to convince your care receiver to seek help. You do this by explaining that ways exist to cure incontinence or at least to alleviate it. You should mention medication therapy (several families of drugs can help), an exercise program to strengthen the muscles that control urination, a painless method of stimulating those muscles, and surgery. Make an appointment with the family physician, who can explain these methodologies more thoroughly.

If your care receiver does indeed seek help and is prescribed a combination of medication and exercises, suggest that the exercises—which involve alternately tightening and relaxing the muscles that control urine flow—be done at certain times each day. This makes it easier to remember to do them.

A wide range of products is available to help manage incontinence, the most comon being padded undergarments and (for males) drip collectors. Make sure your care receiver is aware of the range and, perhaps with the family physician's help, selects the most appropriate product.

Osteoporosis

Osteoporosis is characterized by decreasing bone mass: bones can become so weakened in severe cases that a hug or a cough can break a rib. Many more women than men develop this condition.

Make sure your care receiver has an exercise program developed for her or him by a qualified health professional. Then make sure she or he follows the program on a regular basis. Movement is essential. Failure to move or to exercise weakens already fragile bones. Also advise your care receiver to walk tall, not stooped, and to sit upright in a comfortable armchair that provides good support for the spine.

If your care receiver's osteoporosis is relatively severe, and if you see this person bending at the waist or twisting the spine, remind her or him that these are dangerous movements that could cause a fracture, and that there are better ways to achieve an end. For instance, to get up from a chair, move the buttocks to the edge of the chair and push off with the hands, keeping the back straight at all times. Similarly, the safest way to turn over in bed is to roll like a log so that the spine remains straight throughout the movement.

If you notice this person picking up heavy objects, again gently point out that this is dangerous. And since a fall may result in broken bones for someone with osteoporosis, remove—or help your care receiver to remove—any likely causes of falls around the house. These include scatter rugs on polished surfaces, loose floor tiles, low-level objects such as footstools, frayed carpeting and electrical cords left on the floor. Make sure stairwells and hallways are well lit. Also encourage your care receiver to wear nonskid shoes with low heels.

Parkinsons

Believed to be caused by an insufficiency of dopamine, a chemical in the brain, Parkinsons causes tremoring, bodily rigidity, difficulty in balancing and slowness of movement. Some people with Parkinsons also find that they speak less clearly and more softly, and that they have difficulty in swallowing.

Several types of medication alleviate symptoms, and your first task is to ensure that your care receiver takes medications as prescribed. As well, the family physician will most likely refer this person to one or more therapists who will design a suitable exercise program to promote balance and good posture and to improve general physical skills and hand and finger dexterity. Ensure that this exercise program is followed regularly.

People with Parkinsons often become depressed. If this happens to your care receiver, remember that keeping busy with jobs and other activities can be a salvation for depressed people. If the depression is serious and prolonged, antidepressant medication, which some-times also helps to alleviate the symptoms of Parkinsons, will prob-ably be needed. You'll find more counsel on coping with depression in Chapter Nine.

Remember that slower movement is a symptom of Parkinsons. Be patient when your care receiver takes far more time than previously to perform an action such as climbing the stairs or dressing. Even simple tasks, such as raising a fork to the mouth, may take longer.

To combat hand tremoring, suggest your care receiver use a straw when drinking, or fill a cup or glass half full instead of to the brim, or use a cup with a partial lid. Rubber placemats will prevent plates and bowls from moving about. Many specialty kitchen stores sell cutlery with special handles designed for those with disabilities.

Bathroom safety is important. Encourage your care receiver to use grab bars and rubber mats.

Both Parkinsons and medications to treat it can help cause consti-pation, so make sure your care receiver ingests sufficient fibre and drinks plenty of liquids. Exercise is also helpful.

If your care receiver has difficulty swallowing, encourage him or her to choose moist, soft foods and to have small meals up to six times daily instead of three large meals.

Stroke

A stroke occurs when the brain becomes starved of blood, due either to a clot in an artery or to a cerebral hemorrhage, and in consequence many of the brain's nerve cells die. Since nerve cells control move-ment, part of the body may become paralyzed. The stroke victim may also have difficulty in speaking, writing or reading. Memory may also be impaired.

If the right side of your care receiver's brain was damaged by a stroke, the left side of her or his body will be weakened, and vice versa. A prime task for you is to encourage this person not to forget the weaker side and instead to move and exercise it. Sit on the weaker side while conversing, pass objects to her or him from that side.

As with Parkinsons and any other condition that impairs movement, bathroom safety, provided by grab bars and rubber mats, is vitally important. Until all limbs are functioning normally, don't leave your care receiver alone in the bathroom. Even then, keep a bell or other noisemaker in the bathroom as an alarm call for help if it's needed.

Dressing is important. People who have had a stroke often feel as if they are incomplete and have little self-worth. Left to their own devices, they may remain in rumpled nightclothes and slippers and not bother to wash or to comb their hair—all signs that they are ill. Encourage your care receiver to dress and follow normal grooming routines, and in so doing feel more like a well person. If necessary, teach your care receiver how to dress and undress. To dress, lay out clothes in the order in which they'll be put on, then indicate that the weaker limbs go into them first. When undressing, the stronger limbs are removed from clothing first.

Consider buying new clothes or adapting existing ones to make them easier to put on and take off. Velcro closures, snaps and grippers, and elastic waistbands are all helpful to someone who has trouble doing up buttons. Slip-on shoes are a good idea too.

If your care receiver does indeed wear shirts or blouses that button, the best way is to button from the bottom up since this makes putting buttons in the right buttonholes easier.

Your care receiver may have difficulty distinguishing right from left. You might mark the sole of a left shoe with a large L. Also remind this person that watches are worn on the left wrist (except by the left-handed).

If your care receiver has aphasia—partial or total loss of the ability to use words—a speech therapist should be consulted. After running tests, the therapist should then go over this person's communication strengths and weaknesses with you and explain how you can be of help in promoting the return of the ability to use words. Work diligently at this, since getting along with each other and working together will be far easier when you can communicate easily with each other.

If your aphasic care receiver doesn't seem able to understand what is being said, don't assume this to be true. When in her or his presence, never say anything you wouldn't want this person to hear.

If a stroke has caused your care receiver to become confused, issue simple directions when she or he is trying to solve a problem or complete a task. Encourage her or him to repeat a difficult activity; with practice it will become less difficult.

Your care receiver may experience loss of sensation on the weaker side. For this reason, the temperature of water should always be tested by the hand of the good side.

People whose ability to move easily has been impaired by a stroke are subject to falls. For this reason, you should follow the guidelines for "fall-proofing" the home outlined in the previous section on osteoporosis.

Stroke victims who exercise regularly two or three times a day usually recover faster than those who don't, all other things being equal. If your care receiver has not received a set of recommended exercises, ask the family physician, who will probably give a referral to a therapist. Then make sure recommended exercises are done regularly.

One study has shown that stroke patients who receive strong support from family members and friends are likely to recover lost abilities faster and more permanently than are patients who receive little or no support. So be supportive of your care receiver. Offer help but don't be overprotective; this person has to move and exercise and try to do things without help at least sometimes. Be patient and encourage her or him to practise difficult tasks.

Vision Loss

Improved medications and surgical techniques have helped numerous elders who would otherwise have experienced severe vision loss due to such conditions as glaucoma and cataracts, but there are still more than half a million Canadians who are blind or who have serious vision loss—and many very elderly people whose caregivers must take special precautions if they are not to fall or otherwise injure themselves or break things.

Make sure stairways are well lit, and use bright reflective tape on the edges of the treads.

Use contrasting colors in contrasting densities. If broadloom and upholstery in a room are both pale green, someone with severe vision impairment may have difficulty discerning furniture. If chairs or a loveseat are covered with, say, big-pattern throws, they will be far easier to see.

"Fallproof" the home as described in the section on osteoporosis. And don't move pieces of furniture without telling your care receiver and indicating the new positions. A fall because a favorite chair has been moved or because of a trip over a footstool in a new position could do serious damage.

Use paint or tape in a contrasting color and density along the edges of kitchen and bathroom counters. This will help ensure your care receiver doesn't miss the counters and drop things on the floor.

If your care receiver has sufficient vision to do some writing—letters perhaps—use bright task lighting falling on a dark surface, which will contrast well with a sheet of white paper. Use paper with bold lines, and a magnifying device on a stand so that it does not have to be held in the hand.

If your care receiver enjoys cooking and uses the oven a lot, glue little raised markers onto the dial at temperatures often used—say 250° F and 350° F.

Don't use clear glass dishes or tumblers. Your care receiver will probably not be able to perceive them.

Some good holiday or birthday gifts for a person with severely impaired vision: a talking clock, a talking watch, a talking weight scale, a timer that rings when the time is up (perhaps your care receiver must take medication one hour after a meal, or wants to listen to a radio program starting in half an hour), a pack of playing cards with very large numbers.

Here's More Help

Parkinsons: The Complete Guide for Patients and Caregivers, by Dr. Abraham Lieberman, is available from the Parkinson Foundation of Canada, 390 Bay St., Suite 710, Toronto, M5H 2Y2, at a cost of $14 (this includes shipping and taxes).

The Canadian Hearing Society sells several units helpful for those with impaired hearing. The Call Alert flashes a lamp hooked up to it when the telephone rings, and works both when the lamp is switched on and when it is switched off. It costs $45. The Super Phone-Ringer is promoted as the loudest telephone ringer available, generating up to 95 decibels of sound. Its volume is adjustable. It costs $49. The Alertmaster is the Cadillac of signalling devices. When the telephone rings, or someone knocks on the front door, or the alarm clock goes off, or other sounds are heard such as a baby's cry, the device works in three ways: it flashes a lamp hooked up to it, it shakes a bed (to waken the sleeping user) and it activates a panel of lights that indicate the cause of the alert. It costs $260. Contact the Canadian Hearing Society at 3034 Palstan Rd., Suite 201, Mississauga, Ont., L4Y 2Z6.

Living with Vision Loss: A Handbook for Caregivers is available, at a cost of $12.50, from the Canadian National Institute for the Blind, 1929 Bayview Ave., Toronto, M4G 3E8.

Just about all the organizations that exist to help people with specific physical conditions have written or video material that would be helpful to caregivers. For instance, if your care receiver has diabetes, contact the local branch of the Canadian Diabetes Association.

CHAPTER NINE

Coping With Common Psychiatric Problems and Aberrant Behaviors

"It is pretty hard to watch someone die a little every day—especially when it is someone you love."

Torontonian Ivy St. Lawrence, for many years an activist and a volunteer campaigner for elders, is recalling the years she was the caregiver to her husband Tom, who had Alzheimers. The little daily deaths were the worst part of the experience, she says.

Another bad part, she recalls, was losing friends. "First of all, where you had foursomes he could no longer be part of the group, so you lose that. Then I couldn't leave him alone unless I got a babysitter, so I had to stay in with him. Then friends became embarrassed when he got mixed up, so they didn't come around any more. So you find yourself just about as lonely as a person can be."

Now 83, Ivy has had a double experience of giving care to someone with Alzheimers; she looked after her father when he had it. Asked whether she felt resentful when her husband also developed the condition and she realized she had to live through looking after an

Alzheimers patient all over again, she says emphatically, "No. There was no question that I was not going to look after him because I loved him very dearly and he me." In fact, she looked after him for nine years until she realized she no longer had the health or the stamina to keep watch over him 24 hours a day. So he spent the last two years of his life in a home.

Despite the sad memories, Ivy says she was lucky in at least one respect. Many Alzheimers patients develop changes in behavior, becoming hostile and even physically violent, but Tom never did. "He was a very, very loving person and that stayed with him. When he didn't know who I was, he proposed to me! Three times altogether! He would say, 'Will you do me the honor of being my wife?' and I would bow gravely and say, 'I would be delighted to be your wife.' Right up to the last he demonstrated his love for me."

Ivy has another funny memory. At one point, she was going out to work and had hired a housekeeper. One day when she came in, the housekeeper said to her, "I don't know what to do about your husband," and when Ivy asked what the problem was, she replied, "He gift-wraps the garbage."

"I don't know why Tom had this mania for gift-wrapping garbage," Ivy says. "But we let him go ahead. That and doing the dishes gave him something to do. The garbage men must have thought we were mad!"

Ivy has indeed been lucky—in more ways than one. She has a fine sense of humor, which doubtless helped her survive perhaps the most difficult role for a caregiver: looking after someone who has Alzheimers or any other type of dementia.

Just as the last chapter explored what extra efforts caregivers may have to make when looking after people with specific physical conditions, this one will examine what is involved in giving care to people with specific psychiatric conditions, among them dementia, and to people with behavioral problems.

Depression

Between 10% and 15% of people over the age of 65 have some symptoms of depression, but only 2% to 3% have full-blown clinical depression. An elder often suffers from depressive symptoms after the death of a partner, a condition that is a reaction to a distressing event, and that may diminish with the passage of time.

If your care receiver is indeed depressed because of the recent death of a partner, he or she needs to experience affection. So express your love in words and gestures often. A big hug will probably be welcome. It may, however, generate a flood of tears. Anyone who has just been widowed has a need to express feelings of great sorrow, so don't say, "Try not to cry." Instead, let this person know you understand how upset he or she must be feeling.

As you'll recall, you learned what are the symptoms of depression in Chapter Five. If your care receiver displays any of these symptoms, contact the family physician without delay. The physician may refer your care receiver to a psychiatrist. Almost certainly the physician or the psychiatrist will prescribe one of several antidepressant medications that are effective in treating depression.

Under no circumstances should you tell someone suffering from depression to "snap out of it, you have a good life." Depression is not just a state of mind or a mood. People who are depressed have been shown to have abnormal levels of certain chemicals in the brain. Since they can't control the levels of those chemicals, they can't regulate their depressed feelings. Indeed, antidepressant medications work by modifying the changed levels of brain chemistry.

Don't be critical of a depressed person. People who are depressed often already feel that they are inadequate or failures.

Depressed people are often irritable and easily annoyed, and this may cause you to feel irritable too. Try to recognize when you feel annoyed and try to be patient, because the irritability is a reflection of the depression.

Depressed people often seem to become self-centred and want to talk about how they feel. If your care receiver does this, again be patient. Listen, and make sure this person knows you are listening by looking at him or her during the conversation. Listening, rather than offering solutions to this person's problems, may be your most important contribution, since it enables you to better understand the sufferer's feelings, and hence helps you to empathize.

People who are depressed sometimes wish others would just leave them alone. If this is true of your care receiver, don't insist on social contact. But look in on the sufferer from time to time and ask, "Is there anything I can do for you?"

Don't baby the depressed person or try to do everything for him or her. Activity or occupation of some sort is beneficial for depressed people, as it diverts the mind from thoughts of sadness or inadequacy.

Encourage the depressed person to do some aerobic exercises—walking, swimming or working out on a stationary bicycle or tread-mill perhaps. As you already know, such exercise increases one's sense of well-being by promoting a greater flow of beneficial brain chemicals.

The depressed person probably has little or no interest in sexual relations. If this person is your partner, don't take a change of interest as a reflection on you. Depression has this effect on many people. There are many other ways of expressing affection, including a hug.

Plan special activities you know the depressed person enjoys—a Chinese buffet luncheon next Saturday perhaps, or a visit to a bird-watching area on Sunday afternoon. Plan together a little while ahead; the anticipation may prove almost as enjoyable as the activity itself. But don't be discouraged if there is little apparent interest in the planning or even the event.

Also make sure the depressed person continues to take an interest in personal care—washing and dressing for instance—and also continues to indulge in regular activities she or he enjoys—going into the garden to look at the new plantings and to watch the birds at the feeding station, for example.

Encourage your depressed care receiver's friends and acquaintances to telephone. Also encourage them to write or visit.

Finally, look after yourself. Dealing with a depressed person can cause the caregiver to become depressed as well. So take time out for yourself. Make sure you get plenty of exercise and good food. Go out with friends for a meal or other activity from time to time, and don't abandon regular activities such as club meetings. If you don't do these things, you will probably start to resent the depressed person's presence and become hostile—developments that will do neither of you any good.

Bipolar Affective Disorder (BAD)

Carol Thompson recalls several occasions when her manic depressive husband, John, became violent towards her. Once, "he put his hands around my throat and said he was going to choke me—which he started to do. We were babysitting at the time, so I just said, 'John, the children!' I kept my voice level and didn't show him any fear, and I talked him down until he took his hands off my throat."

Once, when John became exceptionally active and hostile, Carol called the police and asked them to take him in until he had calmed down, which they did.

John is not a typical manic depressive patient. Prior to being put on medication, he lived his whole life in a manic phase, whereas most of those who suffer from BAD have wild mood swings—from a highly active manic phase to the other extreme, depression. If this alternation of moods describes the behavior of your care receiver, make an appointment with the family physician as soon as possible because, like depression, BAD responds well to medication.

You already know from the previous section how to respond to your care receiver when she or he is in the depressive phase. When the person is in the manic phase, remain calm, speak normally and do not show fear. If the situation becomes extreme, call on outside help: 911 will bring an ambulance, accompanied by the police.

Carol has another piece of advice. She says, "I am now more understanding, and most times I am more tolerant. A lot of times we forget that it is an illness manifesting itself. We start to put our own feelings ahead of those of the one who is ill, forgetting that he is not in control of what is happening." The realization that this person's abnormal behavior is caused by a serious condition certainly makes for a more tolerant caregiver. And understanding that condition teaches the caregiver how to respond to a crisis.

Dementia, Including Alzheimers

Peggy Flemming was not so fortunate as Ivy St. Lawrence. When the behavior of her husband, Earl, began to change due to Alzheimers, he started to beat her up. "There was an awful lot of violence," she recalls. "He didn't know what was wrong with him. He would apologize the next day." On one occasion he even held a gun to her head.

"It's hard to cope when you wake up and find that the husband you used to talk and laugh with, carry on and go out with, take off for a weekend with—this person is gone, completely gone, and you become an enemy."

Earl, who began to exhibit symptoms of dementia some eight years ago when he was 57, is no longer violent, but there are still arguments. "They're over something silly. If we run out of eggs, bread or peanut butter, there is a big commotion. It's worse than a child, I think, because you can give a child something else. But he won't want a cookie, he wants peanut butter or else!"

Earl is still able to function almost normally. As well as looking after the dog, he vacuums the apartment, does the dishes after meals and prepares his own breakfast. But he is sometimes forgetful. For instance, he may forget to shave. On one occasion, Peggy had bought a whole flat of eggs and, because the kitchen is short on storage space, had put the eggs in the oven, which she seldom uses. She went out, then had a premonition that something might be wrong, so turned around and went home again. Sure enough, Earl had turned the oven on, quite forgetting to look inside first to make sure nothing was in there. He breakfasted off three or four hardboiled eggs for quite a while after that. Fortunately, he does not have a cholesterol problem!

Peggy has sound advice for other people looking after care receivers with dementia. "You have to have an awful lot of patience," she says. "And if you don't have a sense of humor, you're a goner, you're knocking your head against a brick wall. Earl and I both have a sense of humor, and some really funny things happen that we laugh at. It's a great help."

About 8% of people over 65 suffer from some form of dementia. Among the causes are Alzheimers—which afflicts more than 300,000 Canadians and which destroys brain cells—and repeated small strokes. Some people with Parkinsons also experience dementia. Among the symptoms are memory loss, problems with speech and failure to understand the conversations of others. There may be changes in behavior, including confusion and wandering. With the increasing difficulty in comprehending the world around them, there may be agitation and even suspicion.

However, even though your care receiver appears not to understand what other people are saying, you cannot assume this to be true. When you are in this person's presence, never say anything you would not want him or her to hear.

Life will be easier for both you and your care receiver if you can communicate. When doing so, choose an environment where there is little or no background noise, face her or him directly and talk slowly and clearly in a low tone of voice. Keep sentences short and simple, and avoid complicated thoughts or explanations. Where appropriate, use gestures to reinforce what you are saying. You might also use reminder cues, holding out a jacket perhaps as you say, "Time to go for a walk."

When asking a question, make it short, simple and easy to answer. For instance, don't ask "What would you like for lunch?" Instead, ask, "Would you like an omelet for lunch?" Also use affirmative statements. For instance, say, "Here are some absolutely delicious truffles. Would you like one?"

Don't use baby talk when conversing with your demented care receiver. And always consider and respect this person's feelings. If he or she becomes confused over a loss—perhaps a pet cat which has died—empathize, saying sad feelings are fully justified.

Don't feel you have to keep talking. Silences can indeed be golden. You might ask her or him whether holding hands would be enjoyable. If the answer is "Yes," you might hold hands while listening to music or paging through a coffee table book or a magazine. Sitting quietly together can be a form of communication.

Interact often with your care receiver and encourage him or her to respond. If people with dementia don't use what communication skills remain to them, they may lose those skills more rapidly.

Many people with dementia have trouble making decisions and may become angry because they feel overwhelmed when faced with choices. Consequently, don't ask your care receiver what clothes he or she would like to wear today. Instead, simply make the choice and lay the clothes out. At mealtimes, serve casseroles or mixed salads so that your care receiver doesn't have to choose among several vegetables or salad ingredients on the table. Also lay only one piece of cutlery—probably a spoon or a fork—for him or her.

If this person likes to cook, have a microwave oven or one that can be programmed to shut off automatically. Glass doors on cupboards will make location of dishes and utensils easier. If possible, you or someone else should be in the kitchen when your care receiver is cooking, to provide both safety and companionship.

If your care receiver wanders, have an identity bracelet made bearing his or her name, address and telephone number, and make sure it is worn at all times.

Some communities have what is known as a "wandering registry," run jointly by the local branch of the Alzheimer Society of Canada and the police. Entries detail names, addresses and telephone numbers of wanderers, along with physical descriptions and noted behaviors. If your care receiver wanders, ask your local branch of the Alzheimer Society if there is a registry in your area, and if there is, register your care receiver.

Also, let your neighbors and local shopkeepers know that your care receiver suffers from dementia. Ask them to keep an eye open and, if they should see this person walking alone, ask where she or he is going and perhaps say, "Come on in for a short rest," and in either case telephone you right away.

Try to find out why the wanderer wanders. Linda LeDuc, director, support services/education at the Alzheimer Society's national office in Toronto, says, "If someone is heading for the door a lot, try to figure out why. Has this person had enough exercise, or does he just feel a need to take a break? Or is there something driving him—for instance, does he believe he has to go to the office?" You can experiment a little. For instance, go for a walk with him or her to see if this exercise and companionship cures the wandering urge. And your care receiver can probably give you clues in the form of answers to your questions. "The two of you sort of put a puzzle together," LeDuc says. "You end up being a detective most of the time, trying to figure out what it is that is causing the challenging behavior."

Some high-tech devices exist to alert a caregiver that a wanderer is heading out; for instance, doors that trip an alarm when they are opened. LeDuc suggests an easy low-tech alternative. "Disguise the door so this person doesn't know where it is. Hide it behind drapes."

If the wanderer keeps you awake by wandering at night and making a noise, a lack of sleep and being on guard will probably affect your health quite quickly. Consider hiring someone to come in three or four nights a week to look after the wanderer.

To safeguard a night wanderer, lock clothes closets to prevent dressing, and lock all doors to the outside, removing keys. If this person has a habit of turning on taps while wandering, shut off the water valves. All medications, poisonous substances and cleaning and gardening chemicals should be kept behind locked doors at all times in any case.

Make the environment safe for someone with dementia. Have a low bed that's easy to get into and out of. If she or he lives in a two-storey house with a powder room downstairs, consider establishing a bedroom downstairs so that the only time stairs need be negotiated is when taking a bath or shower.

People with dementia should adhere to set routines—mealtimes, for instance—so that they know what to expect and do not become confused. If this person goes for a walk with you, try to walk at the same time each day. A demented person enjoys the familiarity of a regular routine, not least because it gives a sense of security. In a similar vein, do not move furniture or other objects around the house to new positions unless it's absolutely necessary to do so.

If your care receiver has regular tasks to perform, this will impart feelings of responsibility and importance. Perhaps walking the dog in the garden or washing dishes after a meal would be appropriate.

You may notice what is often called the "sundowning effect." Due to this, your care receiver will probably become more confused in the evening and at night. There are several reasons for this. The body's chemistry undergoes changes towards evening. And the reduction of light is associated with changes in body rhythms. As well, the onset of darkness hinders vision. Because of the sundowning effect, tasks requiring clarity of thought should be done early in the day. And during periods of evening confusion, you—or someone else—should be in the room with this person. Don't just sit there watching like a guard, though; engage in some familiar activity such as reading or knitting so that the confused person will feel comfortable with this familiar sight.

If your demented care receiver becomes aggressive or angry, approach slowly and from the front so as not to cause surprise or alarm. Try to calm this person by standing or sitting directly in front of him or her, speaking quietly in a comforting tone.

"Problem-solving skills are very important," Linda LeDuc says. Indeed. If your care receiver is often angry, you must try to discover what causes this annoyance. Being forced to make a choice can engender anger in a person with dementia. So can being made to hurry. So can becoming confused because two people are talking simultaneously. Being overwhelmed in this way can produce a catastrophic reaction.

However, asking this person what causes the anger will probably not be productive. If you do this, you are trying to reason with someone who has probably lost this ability—and indeed, this approach may bring about an episode of anger. Instead, look for repeat patterns of behavior—yours, your care receiver's or anyone else's—that immediately precede outbursts of rage.

As well, look for behaviors or activities that help regain and maintain composure—listening to music perhaps, or sitting in the garden, or going for a walk.

There are other ways you may be able to help your care receiver overcome anger or anxiety or confusion. You might ask this person to try to bring to mind a peaceful and pleasant scene. Slow, deep breathing, drawing air right down into the diaphragm, may have a calming effect once the initial irritability has settled.

Three final thoughts on looking after people with dementia.

One, early on, once the condition is suspected, discuss powers of attorney and decisions regarding care with your care receiver. In brief, a power of attorney is a legal document giving you the right to manage her or his affairs. You'll find a more detailed description of powers of attorney in Chapter Sixteen.

Two, "Get in touch with your local chapter of the Alzheimer Society," Dr. Michael Flynn says. A staff psychiatrist specializing in geriatric care at the Nova Scotia Hospital in Dartmouth, Flynn says people at the society will probably have "innovative and insightful solutions to various problems you may have not even thought about. Respite care can also be arranged through the society. If you are providing all this care without respite, the chances of your burning out are pretty high."

As well, Flynn says, being on call all the time for a patient with dementia makes caregivers feel resentful sooner or later. And then they feel guilty about resenting their care receiver. "So having someone who can take the burden from you, even if it is just for an hour or two in the afternoon a couple of times a week, means you have time to recharge your batteries. You benefit, and the care you are providing is better, so the patient benefits too."

Finally, do not feel guilty if you can no longer look after a demented care receiver and have to resort to institutional care. "We always tell people that long-term care facilities are a part of the Alzheimers continuum," Linda LeDuc says. "Because of the nature of the disease, it is almost impossible for a family member to keep someone at home throughout its course.

"I have never met anyone who has felt comfortable at having to put a relative in a home. It is a very painful experience. So we try right from the beginning to get people to realize it is acceptable to place someone in a care facility."

Acute Confusion

Elders who have acute confusion, also known as delirium, cannot concentrate, think clearly or remember events. Unlike dementia, which usually develops slowly over a period of several years and which is not reversible, acute confusion comes on quickly over a period of hours or days and is often temporary, lasting a few days or maybe a few weeks.

Symptoms of acute confusion include failing to recognize people or misidentifying people, mixing up the past with the present, experiencing hallucinations, holding delusional beliefs ("Someone is trying to poison me") and becoming disoriented. Some elders with acute confusion become aggressive and noisy, while others become quiet and withdrawn. Some may become physically aggressive when approached. Others are misunderstood and are experienced as being hostile.

Acute confusion often has a physical cause. For instance, disorders of the heart, liver, lungs and kidneys can alter the body's chemistry, which in turn can cause acute confusion. So can diabetes or any infection present in the body, as well as some medications, among them tranquilizers, drugs used by people with epilepsy and Parkinsons, sleeping pills and allergy remedies. Elders who have undergone surgery often experience acute confusion, since their nervous systems are more sensitive to the effects of anaesthetics and painkillers.

If your care receiver suddenly develops symptoms of acute confusion, consult the family physician immediately. Acute confusion is often the first indication that the person has developed an infection or some other change in physical condition.

Elders who develop acute confusion may have to be admitted to hospital for a thorough physical examination to detect the under-lying cause. As the primary caregiver, you should inform the hospital staff of the previous health history of the patient, including all ill-nesses and surgery, and any conditions currently present. Tell staff about the patient's usual personality, hobbies, interests, eating and sleeping routines, normal intake of tea, coffee, and alcohol and smoking habits. Also show staff all medications, both prescribed and over the counter, the patient now uses or has used in the recent past.

If eyeglasses and/or a hearing aid were left behind when the patient was admitted, make sure someone brings them in soon. Impaired sight or hearing will only add to the confusion. Give the glasses and/or hearing aid to a staff member as the patient may need help in using them.

If possible, make sure someone familiar is with the patient through the night for the first three or four nights in hospital, as elders with acute confusion may experience the sundowning effect described in the preceding section on dementia. If you have to work the following day, maybe several of you can divide the night up into two- or three-hour shifts. If you don't have to work next day, find someone to come in the second night so you don't become completely exhausted.

Visit often during the day for short periods, and don't bring more than one person with you. A crowd will only increase the confusion. Ask if you may bring in favorite foods, or visit at mealtimes so you can encourage your care receiver to eat.

If the patient misidentifies people, encourage everyone to say who they are as they arrive for a visit, and as they return to the room after being absent for a short while.

In general, when approaching and talking to an elder with acute confusion, follow the guidelines given in the section on dementia.

Once the underlying condition has been diagnosed and treated, the acute confusion may disappear and the patient may still be able to live independently. If this person recalls the confused period and wants to talk about it, let him or her do so. But more usually there is little to recall because the impaired memory is part of the picture. Often there is some recollection of the prevailing anxiety and a sense of something being wrong, but few details.

Memory Loss

Although they often remember events that took place long ago with great clarity, older people often have an accentuation of the customary short-term memory impairment. If your care receiver's memory is very poor, several courses of action suggest themselves.

Dr. Michael Flynn recommends writing down all the things that must be done on any given day—either in a notebook or on a calendar with a large space for each day. Your care receiver should consult the list at the same time each day. "The big thing is making it routine," Flynn says. "You might link it to breakfast perhaps. If it is a routine, a person is less likely to forget to consult the list. It becomes part of a schedule. Eventually people do it without even thinking about it."

Or, if your care receiver's memory is extremely poor, you might recommend that he or she refer to the planning diary several times a day, using an alarm clock as a reminder when it's time to consult the diary. The last consultation should be in the evening, when he or she will review the events of the day, thereby increasing the likelihood of being able to remember them tomorrow.

Ensure that your care receiver has kitchen appliances that turn off automatically—an oven with a timer or a microwave oven—so that she or he won't forget and overcook food. So that recipe ingredients are not left out or added in twice, lay out all the ingredients in their measured amounts in advance.

If your care receiver is confused over paying bills, maybe losing them or forgetting whether they have been paid, obtain a file folder,

write BILLS in large letters on the front of it and leave it in a prominent place, indicating to your care receiver that all bills should be put
into it. Then, every time a bill is paid, he or she should write PAID
across it, also in large letters.

People with memory loss are often embarrassed at their inability
to remember things. So try not to ask questions your care receiver
may not be able to answer. By the same token, you could always leave
today's newspaper in a prominent place so that this person can look
at it and know instantly that today is Monday the 22nd. As well, bring
naturally into conversations past or forthcoming events she or he
may have forgotten all about.

And, of course, don't say, "You said that already." Ask other people
not to say it too. If your care receiver must take medication, buy a
dosette, a pill dispenser marked with indications as to when contents
must be taken. Or you might buy one that beeps when it is time to
take the next dose. Or buy a more sophisticated one. "Some of them
are very high tech," Flynn says. "They have different beeps, one for
your eight o'clock pill and another for your noon pill. All these new
developments are very helpful for older people."

Aberrant Behaviors

"Anger is a big part of her life. She strikes out at me. I had to lock her
out of my office last week—she was getting too aggressive."

Henry Ficke is talking about his wife. She has Huntington's disease,
which is the reason for her aggressive behavior. In their late 50s, the
Fickes live in Kelowna, B.C., where, after taking early retirement from
his company, Henry began working out of his home on contract for
his former employer.

Despite the fact that he feels "very dedicated to her," Henry becomes
upset when his wife vents her anger on him. Her physical condition is

deteriorating, which he also finds upsetting. But, because, he has done the right thing, he is still able to take caregiving in his stride.

"The right thing" was realizing that he had to take care of himself because if he was not in good shape, he would not function well as a caregiver. His first move was to seek counsel from a social worker. His second, when the social worker told him she saw signs of depression in him, was to obtain a prescription for a mild antidepressant drug.

He also has a close involvement with a caregivers' support group in Kelowna, which is helping him. And he is not too proud to accept help in the form of daycare for his wife at a health centre nearby, and respite care, during which someone else comes in to be with his wife while he takes a break. As well, he says, his youngest daughter pitches in willingly; for instance, last year she came up from the B.C. coast to collect her mother, who stayed with her for a couple of weeks.

If your care receiver suddenly develops a problem behavioral trait, a visit to the family physician is in order. A condition such as depression can drastically change the way a person behaves. "If this person is depressed, you treat the depression and very often these behaviors disappear," says Isabelle Everett, a gerontological nurse who works in the Alzheimer Society's branch in Hamilton, and is also president of the Gerontological Nursing Association at time of writing.

Everett also points out that if an older person is depressed or demented, you cannot use the same methods to counter problem behaviors. Indeed, you will almost certainly need professional help of some kind. What follows, therefore, is based on the assumption that these behaviors are being manifested by older people who are cognitively intact and do not suffer from either depression or dementia.

Caregiver Abuse

Some elders become angry because of their disabilities and take their anger out on the nearest target—the primary caregiver. Abuse may be physical, emotional or financial. One example of emotional abuse is shouting loudly at caregivers for making inconsequential mistakes. One example of financial abuse is withholding money needed to cover caregiving expenses.

If the abuse has been happening over a long period, probably partly because you and your care receiver don't really like each other, you won't be able to stop it, Everett says. She recommends you find a support group to belong to, so you can ask other people how they cope with similar situations. "You may even benefit from professional help," she adds.

Aggression and Anger

Don't tell your care receiver not to be angry, as suppressed anger can lead to depression. Instead, give this person every chance to ventilate anger constructively. Ask what is the source of the anger. You'll probably be told declining abilities or increasing disabilities are its source. If so, reply that being angry for this reason is perfectly understandable and normal. Now that your care receiver has vented her or his anger and been told that the reasons for the anger are totally valid, the anger may diminish or disappear altogether.

If you are being attacked verbally, don't become emotional and don't fight back. Listen to what is being said and if you hear anything that is true—perhaps you *were* a trifle hasty in clearing the table when there was still some tea in your care receiver's cup—agree and, if appropriate, apologize. This, probably the last thing your attacker expected, will give him or her pause.

Extreme Dependence

Some elders feign helplessness in order to draw attention to themselves. But catering to their every whim is not a good idea. They should be encouraged to do things for themselves, then praised for their achievements.

For instance, your care receiver may ask you to cut up food, pleading arthritic fingers. But you know the arthritis is not severe enough to prevent the cutting of food. Say something like, "Try cutting up soft things first—the potato maybe . . . Great, you did that just fine. Now try cutting the meat . . . There, see, you can manage really well on your own. Well done!"

Power Plays

Older people quite often try to force their caregivers to do unnecessary things for them. What they are trying to do is show that they still call the shots around here. Isabelle Everett provides an example.

"Say, for instance, your mother lies in bed and wants breakfast brought in every morning, though there is nothing physically or mentally wrong with her. You decide that breakfast is going to be served in the kitchen. So you say, 'If you would like breakfast, come and join us in the kitchen. Otherwise there is no breakfast.'

"Then, the day when she does get up and join you, you praise her to the hilt. 'It's wonderful to have you here, I'm so glad you decided to do this. It's going to be really great having breakfast together.'"

As another example, Everett cites a mother who doesn't want what's being served for dinner and instead wants something cooked specially for her. "You don't become a short-order cook," Everett says, even if your mother complains of hunger half an hour later.

Everett has one caveat. Don't try to change two undesirable behaviors at the same time. In other words, using the two examples just given, until your mother becomes a regular at the breakfast table let her have her way at dinner.

Denial of Reality

Older people quite commonly deny that they feel unwell or are unable to do things when they do in fact not feel well and have difficulty doing certain things.

Your first task is to persuade the elder to admit to the reality. You might, for instance, comment on the fact that this person is moving more stiffly than usual and simultaneously grimacing a little. Once you have managed to get a person to admit to the discomfort, say something warm and encouraging. Try a comment such as "Thanks for leveling with me. I really appreciate it because I know then when I should be around to help you and when I can go out shopping and leave you here without worrying."

Sometimes you may have to call on outside help to get someone to accept reality. Many elders will accept the judgment of a doctor or nurse. "Doctor, please put on your white coat and hang your stethoscope around your neck and tell my mother she's not well enough to go home yet" may produce the desired result.

Hypochondria

Someone who complains of aches and pains all the time is not unlike the extremely dependent person. The complaints are really cries for attention, and efforts must be made to distinguish between real problems and imaginary ones.

This calls for a conversation marked by good communication. For instance, say your father is complaining bitterly about the arthritis in his hips. Ask him to be specific about where he feels the pain. Ask him to stand and walk a little way, describing to you how he feels as he does so. If you think he is affecting a limp or exaggerating how he feels by walking extremely slowly, ask whether he can walk faster and more upright. Say it would make you happy if he could move more easily. Chances are, when he hears you say that, he will move more easily.

If the complaints go on and on, day after day, you should tell this person that constant complaints just aren't acceptable in this household and, while you will listen and empathize for, say, 10 minutes a day, that is the limit. Be polite but firm. As Everett says, "You were never meant to be a doormat."

Alcoholism

Alcoholism is a disease, and no amount of behavior management will help you if your care receiver has this problem. This person needs professional help. But if he or she drinks heavily but is not yet a full-blown alcoholic, you may be able to be of some assistance.

Choose a time when your care receiver has not been drinking and there are no outside distractions. Say that you have learned some alarming facts about the effects of alcohol on the body and the brain, and that you are concerned that he or she may be drinking enough to do harm. Never use the word "alcoholic." Ask whether a visit to the family physician to discuss alcohol usage might not be a bad idea, and offer to go along if desired.

Quitting drinking altogether may be an unrealistic goal if the care receiver is very elderly and does not expect to live long. One organization, Community Older Persons Alcohol Program, or COPA, in Toronto, believes that for such people reduced consumption is a more realistic and more acceptable goal.

In many cases, and not just that of heavy drinking, a total change of a problem behavior may not be possible, and moderation of the behavior may be more attainable.

Here's More Help

A series of videotapes developed by a team of researchers at the University of Utah provides a break for caregivers who look after people with dementia. Appropriately entitled Video Respite, the tapes are designed to hold the attention of people with dementia and have them react at times, perhaps mimicking the movements of the person they see on the screen, perhaps singing along to some old favorite tunes. Meantime, the caregiver can safely leave the room. There are generalized tapes, such as *Remembering When,* a program that reminisces about early life experiences such as school and picnics, and *Gonna Do a Little Music,* in which a woman plays the guitar and autoharp and asks viewers to sing along and do some simple exercises. There are also specialized tapes, among them one aimed primarily at women, another primarily for men, yet another primarily for Jewish people, and one for African North Americans. The tapes vary in length, from 22 to 55 minutes. For more information about Video Respite, contact Innovative Caregiving Resources at P.O. Box 17332, Salt Lake City, UT 84117-0332, U.S.A.

CHAPTER TEN

Caring for Confined Elders

A good many of the caregivers interviewed while researching material for this book were or are looking after people partially or wholly confined to bed or to a wheelchair.

For instance, Nicole Charron, a Montrealer, looked after her partner, Keith, for two years until his death. Keith had amyotrophic lateral sclerosis, a neuromuscular disease that renders muscles increasingly useless. "The thing he found the hardest was not walking," Nicole recalls. "He used to say, 'If only I could get out of this chair and walk!' Once, he had a dream in which he was standing and walking. I am sure that dream was a sign from the Lord. He had it about a week or so before he died. By then, I saw that he was deteriorating so fast that his death would be a blessing."

In the early months, Nicole was able to help Keith move from place to place unaided, but later on she had to use a lift. Caring for someone who is partially or wholly confined to bed or to a wheelchair often calls for assistive devices such as lifts and special techniques. In this chapter we'll take a look at some of each.

Bathing

First, some general rules about bathing, no matter whether your care receiver can do it alone or whether you are helping.

Don't let an elderly person stay in the tub for more than 20 minutes. Prolonged soaking leads to dry skin and, as you'll recall from Chapter Four, many elders have dry skin.

Use warm water, never hot. Very hot water washes off the body's natural oils and can also lead to dry skin.

Use a good glycerine-based or superfatted soap. Soap hands, armpits and the genito-rectal area daily, the rest of the body only once or twice a week.

To combat dry skin, use a good moisturizer after bathing. You might ask the family physician for a recommendation. Or you might use baby oil; it's both effective and inexpensive.

If your care receiver isn't too steady when standing, you should have a clamp-on safety rail installed on the side of the bathtub, and a grab bar on the wall beside the tub. The user then puts one hand on the rail and one on the bar when getting into and out of the tub.

For those even less steady on their feet, a whole range of bath benches and seats exists. At the simplest end of the range is an adjustable bath bench which stretches from one side of the bath to the other. The user sits on the bench, steadies himself or herself by holding onto a bar or rail and lifts one leg at a time into the bath. The bench also doubles as a seat while showering. At the more complex end is a wide chair, two of whose legs sit outside the bath, while the other two are in the bath. The user sits outside the bath, then moves along the seat, lifting legs one at a time, until directly over the bath. Some chairs have a hole in the seat to facilitate washing of the genito-rectal area.

There are lifts for use in a tub. One kind is secured to the bottom of the tub by four suction cups. The user sits in it, and the seat then slides down until the user is in the water and almost sitting on the bottom of the tub. The seats of some models swivel to make getting into and out of the bath easier. Most of these lifts are hydraulically powered.

When bathing your care receiver, wash in this order: face, neck and arms, torso, legs, feet.

Have this person stand, supported if necessary, so you can wash the genito-rectal area, always washing from front to back to prevent bacteria from finding their way from the rectum to the urinary tract.

Drain out the water and start to dry your care receiver when she or he is still in the tub. Dry hands well; wet hands may slip on a bar or rail. Help this person out of the bath and onto a chair. Wrap her or him in a large bathsheet for warmth. Finish drying. Use talc or cornstarch between the toes and other places where two skin surfaces meet, such as the armpits.

Showering

Your care receiver prefers a shower to a bath? Follow the same procedure, washing the body in the same order as above. If the shower is in a separate stall, this too should be fitted with grab bars.

Unless they have some disability of the arms or hands, elders usually find a hand-held shower head easier to use than a fixed one, since they can stand still while rinsing soapsuds off.

Incidentally, if your care receiver feels embarrassed at appearing naked while being helped by you, turn on a radio and discuss what you are both hearing, or play some music you know he or she likes in a nearby room. Or just generally chat and elicit responses to your questions.

Sponge Bathing

For anyone who can't bath or shower and who must be sponge bathed, there are two ways to go.

143

The first is when your care receiver can do some of the work. Here's how to proceed, step by step.

1. This person sits on the edge of the bed with feet hanging down over the side. Put a blanket over the lower torso and legs for warmth, and towels or incontinence pads under and around the body to keep bedclothes dry.
2. Help your care receiver out of pyjama or nightgown top if necessary. He or she then washes and dries face, neck, arms, upper torso and abdomen.
3. Drape the blanket over the upper body for warmth. Help this person to remove nightgown or pyjama bottoms. You wash and dry legs and feet.
4. Have your care receiver lie down on one side. Use the blanket to keep legs warm. Protect the bedclothes with a pad or towels.
5. You wash and dry the back and buttocks.
6. If this person can't wash the genito-rectal area, have him or her roll over until face up, enabling you to do the job.
7. Help him or her to dress.
8. Position this person sitting on the edge of the bed, legs over the side, feet in a basin of warm water. Let feet soak for two or three minutes, then wash and dry them.

Incidentally, having a bed the right height—level with your waist—will make it easier for you to work with your care receiver without placing a strain on your back. If the bed is too low, and you don't want to go to the expense of buying a new one, remove wheels if the legs have them and put wooden blocks under the legs.

If your care receiver is incapacitated and can't help or sit up, here's how you proceed.

1. Position towels or pads to shield the bedclothes. Cover this person with a blanket for warmth. Remove pyjama or night-gown top and drape a towel over the chest.
2. Wash face and ears and dry both thoroughly.
3. Wash and dry the front and sides of the neck, then hands and arms, using long, slow strokes from wrists up to shoulders.
4. Remove the towel and wash and dry chest and underarms.
5. Put the towel back over the chest. Remove pyjama or night-gown bottom and wash abdomen and groin area.
6. Cover the torso with the blanket for warmth, then wash legs, again using long strokes and working from ankles up to groin.
7. If this person can't sit on the edge of the bed, put a bowl with a little water in it, and plenty of protection under it, on the bed and have him or her bend the knees and soak the feet in the bowl for two or three minutes. Wash and dry feet.
8. Have this person turn over onto one side. Wash and dry the back of the neck and shoulders, back and buttocks.
9. Have this person lie face up. Wash and dry genito-rectal area.

Shaving

If you must shave your care receiver, and if you have never shaved anyone before, ask an experienced person to show you how.

If your care receiver takes an anticoagulant drug (it prevents blood from clotting), he—or you if you shave him—should use an electric razor to prevent nicks and consequent blood flows.

Hairwashing

If you are washing your care receiver's hair in a vanity basin, have this person face the basin and lean forward. Do not have her face away from the basin and lean back: this latter position, if maintained for some time, may interfere with the blood supply to the brain, which in turn may cause dizziness or other unpleasant sensations.

If your care receiver is bedridden, you might use an inflatable vinyl shampoo basin, which supports a user's neck and shoulders. It inflates by mouth or pump and comes complete with drain hose.

If you find hairwashing to be a rigorous experience for both of you, ask the family physician whether you might use a dry shampoo on an occasional basis.

Moving a Confined Person

If you can find someone willing to help you, try these moves first on a healthy person, repeating them until you have the hang of them.

First, let's suppose you want to move your care receiver from a lying position to a sitting one. Turn this person onto one side and facing you, and fairly close to the edge of the bed. Now help her or him to bend the legs at the knee, then swing them over the side of the bed. Put your arm around your care receiver's shoulders and gently pull until she or he is sitting upright.

To move someone from a bed to a chair, first make sure you are both wearing nonskid footwear. Perform the manoeuvre described in the previous paragraph to position your care receiver sitting on the edge of the bed. Determine whether this person has a stronger side by asking her or him to grasp your hands and squeeze hard. If the right side is stronger, place a chair to her or his right.

Ask this person to rotate the feet and wiggle the toes to get the circulation in the feet going. Next, stand close in so that your knees are touching. Maintain this knee contact throughout the move to prevent your care receiver's knees from buckling.

Bend forward and ask this person to lock hands around your neck or shoulders. Put your arms around her or his waist. Slowly straighten your back, bringing her or him up with you. Stand still with your arms around each other for a minute or so, to ward off dizziness. Then slowly turn this person to the right so that she or he is close to the chair, and able to use the right (good) arm to gain stability as you slowly lower her or him into the chair.

If your care receiver wants to walk across the room and needs your help, stand on the weaker side—if there is one—and put your arm around her or his waist or upper back.

Someone using a cane should hold it in the hand of the stronger side.

Lifting and Moving: Assistive Devices

The medical people who came into Carmelle Harrison's home failed to tell her that she could obtain a lift to help her move her husband from one place to another. So she lifted him manually for seven years and in so doing strained her back—not surprisingly since she was occasionally lifting more than she knew. "Sometimes I was lifting both my husband and the chair he was sitting on because he would hold onto it without my knowing." She describes the lift she finally learned about and obtained as "a wonderful invention," and one that enabled her to move him at will from his bed to a wheelchair or a commode or even out to the garden.

The lift Carmelle used was one of the most versatile models. In this type of lift, the patient is supported by a sling suspended from a four-wheeled device and can thus be moved from one place to another at will. In some cases, the arm that supports the sling is raised and lowered hydraulically; in other cases, the motor is electric.

There are also special-purpose lifts. One is often called a trapeze—which it resembles. It either bolts to the wall over the head of a bed or comes as a free-standing floor model which is positioned behind the bed. The "trapeze" dangles on two chains from an overhead arm. The length of the chains is adjustable. If the trapeze is quite high over the user's head, he or she might sit up and grasp it as a support while swinging from the bed to a chair. If the bar is within the reach of a user lying down, he or she can use it as a support when changing position or moving up or down in the bed.

To save you from straining your back when lifting your care receiver out of a chair, you need a chair whose seat tips forward so that its occupant is tipped onto his or her feet. The arms are powered and move too, so the user is in contact with them at all times and remains stable.

Toileting

If your care receiver has some mobility, you might buy a commode for her or him to keep in the bedroom. Some commodes look like a regular chair until the seat is lifted to reveal the container. If you buy the kind that is obviously a commode, you might want to put it behind a screen, so the user—and visitors—can't see it.

Clean a commode after every use, rinsing thoroughly.

If your care receiver must use a bedpan, perhaps on bad days or during recovery from a stroke, ask the family physician or a nurse to show you how to administer it. Before using a bedpan or urinal (a small container men use when emptying the bladder), immerse them in warm water to warm them, and dry thoroughly.

To clean a chamberpot, bedpan or urinal, and to prevent odors from developing, fill with either baking soda and water or a vinegar-and-water solution and let stand for about half an hour.

Making an Occupied Bed

Here is the step-by-step procedure for changing linens on an occu-
pied bed.

1. Fold the clean sheets lengthwise. The crease will indicate
    where their centre is.
2. Have your care receiver move to the side of the bed away from
    you, back to you.
3. Pull the undersheet out from under the mattress and roll it up
    as close to your care receiver's back as possible.
4. Using the crease as a guideline, position the clean undersheet
    on your side of the bed and tuck it in. Place the other half of
    this sheet as close to your care receiver as possible.
5. Have your care receiver turn over until facing you. With your
    help if necessary, have him or her move over the hump of
    sheets in the centre of the bed and towards the edge of the
    bed nearest to you.
6. Go to the other side of the bed. Remove the old sheet, spread
    and smooth out the clean one and tuck it in.
7. Your care receiver's head is probably not on the pillow, so now
    change the pillowslip.
8. Help your care receiver back to the centre of the bed, and
    change the top sheet.

Preventing Bedsores

You'll recall that Chapter Five set out places on the body where
patches of reddened skin, the first sign of bedsores, are most likely to
appear. You'll also recall bedsores are caused by poor circulation. The
first preventive measure is to make sure your care receiver moves and
changes position often, say every hour, to prevent pressure on the

weight-bearing parts of her or his body from cutting off circulation for long periods. If this person can't move unaided, you will have to help.

Use a good skin lotion (but don't rub it into any reddened areas) or talcum powder; either will decrease friction, and the talc will dry up any perspiration that forms at that point. To ensure talc is not inhaled, don't shake it directly onto the skin. Instead, put some on your hands and distribute it by stroking or lightly patting your care receiver's body.

Make sure sheets are clean and wrinkle-free at all times.

If your care receiver is capable, encourage her or him to do mild exercises in bed—moving, stretching and bending limbs, and so forth—to engender improved circulation.

Another way to increase circulation is to massage around any reddened areas. But do not massage the areas themselves, since doing so would further weaken already weakened skin.

Various aids exist to help prevent bedsores. At the simple, inexpensive end of the scale, you can make little rings of cotton wool and place them under the heels when your care receiver is lying face up.

You can buy sheepskin pads to be placed under the lower back, buttocks and shoulder blades, as well as sheepskin heel and elbow protectors.

You might buy what is known as an "eggcrate mattress," so called because it has ridges and valleys like an eggcrate. Used over a regular mattress, it exerts less pressure on the skin than a regular mattress, and its irregular surface allows air to circulate beneath the user.

Or you might buy water cushions or an entire water mattress, both of which are used over a regular mattress. Any kind of water cushion or mattress exerts less pressure on the skin than a regular mattress.

If, despite all your efforts, an open sore develops, consult the family physician.

Here's More Help

The Canadian Red Cross Society makes available for a small fee lifts, commodes and bedpans. For more details, contact your local branch of the society.

Some members of the Canadian Rehabilitation Council for the Disabled lend assistive aids. Write to the CRCD at 45 Sheppard Ave. E., Suite 801, Toronto, M2N 5W9, for a directory that lists members and the loans they make.

To find companies that retail assistive devices, check out the Yellow Pages under "Home Health Services & Supplies," "Hospital Equipment & Supplies" and "Orthopedic Appliances." In particular, three chain operations carry a wide variety of devices. One is Sears Canada; you'll find assistive aids listed in the company's regular catalogue. Another is MDS Doncaster Home Health Care Centres; to find out if there is one near you, write to the head office at 224 Lesmill Rd., Don Mills, Ont., M3B 2T5. The third is Shoppers Drug Mart Home Health Care Centres; its head office is at 225 Yorkland Blvd., Toronto, M2J 4Y7.

Access Place Canada and the organizations within it—notably the Barrier-Free Design Centre—help people with disabilities in several ways. They consult on home design or redesign to accommodate someone with a disability. They provide information on vaious assistive aids and devices. They have displays of aids and devices, and visitors may try out products to decide whether they want to purchase them or not. Access Place is at College Park, 444 Yonge St., Toronto, M5B 2H4.

CHAPTER ELEVEN

Keeping Your Cool

One woman giving care to a husband who has Alzheimers recalls, "There were times when he did not remember who I was and was hitting me. I wanted to hit him back. But I had enough common sense to distance myself from him. I would go into another room, have tea, perhaps, or pray."

Many caregivers do not distance themselves from the situation, as did this woman. Elder abuse is common. The compilers of one study estimated that some 98,000 Canadian elders living in private homes were abused. And that estimate is probably too low since many of those who are abused remain silent for several reasons: their abusers are family members and they are too ashamed to speak out; many abused elders do not realize they are being abused; people with dementia may be unable to communicate their experiences of being abused; through intimidation, threats, bribes and even physical force, people who are abused may be told to keep the abuse a secret. Indeed, a paper entitled "A Handbook for the Prevention of Family Violence" published by Health and Welfare Canada contains an estimate that up to 2.5 million elderly Canadians may be subjected to domestic abuse.

What is known is that, of those who do speak out and thus become statistics, two out of three are women between the ages of 75 and 85.

What is also known is that, more often than not, those who abuse elders are sons in their 30s, 40s or 50s. They have limited education and are likely to abuse alcohol or other mood-altering substances. They become unemployed and consequently move back into the family home with one or both parents, upon whom they become dependent.

"Abuse may occur for many reasons," Gloria McIlveen, executive director of Alzheimer New Brunswick, notes. "Sometimes, caregivers' exhaustion, frustration, anger, stress or lack of information on how to care properly swells to the point where they lose control of their emotions or behavior. These people really do want to do right by their care recipients, but they cannot cope with all the emotional and financial stress placed on them."

There are four categories of abuse: physical, psychosocial, financial and neglect. There are two sub-categories of neglect: active, in which the caregiver knowingly and deliberately fails to attend to a care receiver's needs, and passive, in which the caregiver doesn't realize she or he is harming a care receiver by failing to attend to certain needs.

Physical Abuse

Some cases of physical abuse are truly horrifying. At Maison Jeanne Simard in Montreal, Canada's first shelter for abused elders, staff member France Cottenoir tells of one 74-year-old woman who was beaten up by her daughter and who was admitted to hospital with broken ribs, a broken arm, a black eye and cigarette burns on her body. The daughter was an alcoholic and was forcing her mother to give her money to buy alcohol.

Cottenoir, sister of and assistant to the shelter's founder Johanne

Cottenoir, says many of those taken in for temporary care at the shelter are both physically and financially abused, often by sons or daughters who want their money to buy either alcohol or drugs. When those using the shelter return to the outside world, a social worker checks up on them periodically to help ensure the pattern of abuse does not resume.

Forms of physical abuse include beating, cutting, burning, slapping, pinching, punching, pushing, pulling hair, shaking, forced feeding, sexual molestation, forced confinement, general rough handling, overmedication, undermedication, using unnecessary physical or chemical restraints (e.g., tying to a chair or dosing with tranquilizers), biting and kicking.

Psychosocial Abuse

The following are all forms of psychosocial abuse: humiliation, intimidation, silence, provoking fear, mocking verbally or with gestures, shouting, scolding, imposed social isolation, withholding of love or companionship and treating an elder like a child. As well, psychosocial abuse may take the form of lack of privacy, failing to permit an elder to make decisions, insulting behavior, bullying, calling names such as Silly Old Fool or Duckie, withholding or falsifying information, threats of abandonment or putting away ("If you don't shut up and eat your supper, I'll put you in the old folks' home") and ignoring an elder when he or she talks to you.

Financial Abuse

According to many people working in the field, financial abuse is the most prevalent kind. "It appears to be one of the more prominent forms of elder abuse," says York Region social worker Mindy Packer-Bloom. "Unemployed children have to turn to their parents to get help to support their own families. Often, seniors are taken into the home because the children need their pension cheques. That is the reality of today's life. We see a lot of children thinking they have rights to their parents' money. Sometimes it's the result of ignorance. They don't even realize that they are being abusive." And criminal as well, since anyone found being financially abusive can be prosecuted.

Forms of financial abuse include wrongful use of a power of attorney, fraud, forgery, extortion, stealing money or pension cheques or other possessions and coercion in the writing of wills. Financial abusers may also force a care receiver to sell personal property to raise money for them, use funds for purposes contrary to the needs or wishes of the care receiver and block access to money or other possessions.

Neglect

"All kinds of people are looking after parents whom they really hate," says Isabelle Everett. "And this opens up the ball game of abuse. There is a lot of abuse by neglect and it is horrendous."

Forms of neglect—which, remember, can be either deliberate or unwitting—include withholding of food or drink, inadequate personal care and hygiene, inadequate environmental care (e.g., bed unmade, floor not swept, room not dusted), lack of supervision and leaving an elder alone for long periods. Other forms of neglect are forced entry into an institution, sensory deprivation (e.g., failing to provide access to music or magazines the care receiver enjoys), failing to give a dependent elder anything she or he needs, withdrawal from social interactions and general lack of attention to health care needs.

Ways to Help Avoid Abuse

Not surprisingly, one of the most common factors that cause abusive behavior by caregivers is a high degree of stress. If you are stressed, Gloria McIlveen cites various ways you can relieve the stress before it drives you to abusive behavior. First, learn to know yourself, to recognize your own strengths and limitations, and find a way of responding to your needs that suits you best. Also, accept others for what they are. You can't change them. And take steps to avoid the danger of burnout—get sufficient sleep, rest, and nourishment and find time for yourself.

Other stress relievers? Call on a family member or neighbor to be with your care receiver while you do something you enjoy. Use the time to get some exercise, garden if you like gardening, go out with a friend for lunch at a restaurant—in short, anything that gives you pleasure.

As well, remind yourself that no one is perfect. You are doing the best you can, and if you make the occasional mistake the world will not come to an end.

Know that many caregivers experience a cocktail of emotions—anger, resentment and guilt among them—often mixed in a solution of exhaustion. If this is how you are feeling, remind yourself that these emotions are entirely normal.

Learn to share these feelings with others—relatives, friends or other caregivers perhaps. Venting is an effective way of reducing stress.

If she or he is not already in one, get your care receiver into a day program to give yourself some time off. Or find out (try the library or the local public health department) whether there are any friendly visitor programs in your area; while a friendly visitor is with your care receiver, you can leave and do something else.

Another way of reducing your stress level is to join a caregivers' support group where you can share experiences and gain knowledge.

Common Characteristics of an Abuser

Abusive caregivers are frequently dependent on the abused person, lacking in social skills, impatient by nature, motivated by financial gain and resentful of the care receiver. If the caregiver has had to give up a job, or even a whole career, in order to provide care, resentment is a trigger of abuse.

Many caregivers become abusive because the role they have taken on has become exceptionally onerous, to the point where they resent and even dislike their care receivers and the demands they make. Commonly, they refuse to seek or accept help in order to lighten the load.

Often, they feel lonely, locked away from the "real" world because of the demands of caregiving. Often, too, they have experienced hardship by taking on the caregiver role. Perhaps the role has proved costly—buying a wheelchair and having to make extensive modifications to the home, for instance—causing financial hardship.

More often than not, there is a history of abusive relationships in the family. Quite often, a caregiver has at one time or another been abused by the care receiver whom he or she is now subjecting to abuse.

Abusive caregivers may boss their care receivers about unnecessarily. They are also apt to blame their care receivers, pointing out such facts as their inability to take a vacation because of caregiving's demands.

Steps for a Potential Abuser to Take

If there is a conflict situation that you feel may lead you to abusive behavior, you need help in resolving the conflict. A sibling may be able to help. If not, you should call in a mediator—perhaps someone from your local family services association. Explain the nature of the conflict, and ask her or him to help you resolve it.

Maybe the problem is that your care receiver is a hypochondriac who complains almost nonstop about largely imaginary aches and pains. When you don't respond every time by sympathizing, this person accuses you of being cold-hearted and not caring "that I'm in terrible pain all the time." You know you're on the verge of shouting, "For crying out loud, shut up!" So you call in your mediator, who instantly recognizes the problem and helps solve it by telling your care receiver that the hypochondriac behavior is stressing you to a dangerous level, and also showing you how to tell your care receiver firmly but politely to complain less.

At all times, if you feel you've lost your cool and are about to abuse your care receiver, immediately talk to someone about it. If no one (other than your care receiver) is present, phone a sibling or a friend to vent your feelings. If you feel you're still in grave danger of losing control, phone your family physician and ask for a referral to an appropriate counselor—probably a social worker.

Examine your own behavior to determine where your flashpoint is—where you become so stressed that you know you will hit out verbally or physically unless you take some action to avoid doing so. Leave the room. Make coffee, water the house plants, read a magazine, call a friend. Take any action that will enable you to catch your emotional breath and become calm again.

CHAPTER TWELVE

Getting Help and Acquiring Skills

"A lifeline" is how Sheila Smythe describes the help family and friendly caregivers receive from homemakers and professional caregivers such as members of the Victorian Order of Nurses. Smythe is a social work supervisor in the Coordinated Client Services Deartment at the Baycrest Centre for Geriatric Care in Toronto, and, as such, knows a great deal about the needs of caregivers. "Sometimes people improve greatly when help is brought in," she says.

Health department supervisor Elizabeth Shantz would agree with Smythe. Her father was rendered paraplegic by an industrial accident at the age of 46. He was cared for by his wife until he was 74. She then sensibly sought help.

As a result, VON personnel came in to give her husband nursing care. As well, homemakers came in to do house cleaning and laundry.

Six years after help started coming in, Shantz's father had to go into acute care. From there he went into chronic care—an event that almost certainly would have happened six years earlier without outside help.

Seeking Nonprofessional Help

Don't hesitate to ask family members and good friends if they will help with activities such as house and yard work, and sitting with your care receiver. Find innovative ways to reward helpers: appropriate gifts such as a gardening book for someone who helps with yard work, or home-baked goodies, or a restaurant meal.

However, don't risk becoming a slave driver. Don't, for instance, tell your nephew, "The lawn needs mowing once a week, so I'll expect you on Saturday mornings." Instead, give him a call when mowing should be done and say, "Any chance you could come around and mow the lawn today or tomorrow?" And if he says no, make clear you don't mind. You'll retain him as a helper far longer that way.

Seeking Professional Help

Many caregivers don't seek help because they don't know how to go about finding it. In fact, there are several ways.

One is to call your local community information centre, or CIC. Staff will know where you can get the kind of help you need. Look in the white pages of the phone book for "Community Information Centre," or "Mytown Information" since the first word of many CICs' titles is the name of the community. If this doesn't yield results, ask a local librarian for the organization's name.

Another way is to ask staff at your local library. Librarians are usually knowledgeable about programs.

Or ask a public health nurse in your local health department, or staff at your local family services association. (Information on how to contact a public health nurse and family services association appears in Chapter One.)

The "Social Services Organizations" section of the Yellow Pages is yet another source of information. In it, you'll find everything from the local branch of the Alzheimer Society and the Family Services Association to Meals on Wheels and the Canadian Red Cross Society, all of which are sources of help.

As well, every province and territory has a handbook, available free of charge, listing and describing services and facilities for elders. Library or CIC staff can tell you how to obtain a copy of the one published by your province or territory.

If you live in Quebec, you can get information and assistance from a Centre Local de Services Communautaires. CLSCs exist in many communities.

Public (i.e., government-run) services cover house and yard work, meal preparation, nursing including foot, hair and skin care, help with bathing and dressing and occupational and physical therapy.

To access public services you need a referral from a family physician or public health nurse. Services are free unless the user exceeds the time period specified by the referral. Beyond that, fees are on a sliding scale so users pay no more than they can afford.

The two largest Canada-wide nonprofit service providers are the Victorian Order of Nurses and the Canadian Red Cross Society.

VON has adult day care centres, which often have special services such as foot care clinics. VON will also send staff into clients' homes. Staff perform a full range of nursing services and in some areas may also provide homemaking services such as meal preparation and light housekeeping.

Not all Red Cross branches provide home care, so check with your local branch by phone. At those that do provide home care, staff will help clients bathe, dress, use the toilet, take meals and so on. They help clients exercise if necessary, and will plan and prepare meals in the home. (They also run Meals on Wheels programs.)

Fees charged by nonprofit services are usually on a sliding scale, so no clients are charged more than they can pay. And if clients have coverage under a provincial or private insurance plan, the plan will probably pay nonprofit services' fees.

You'll find numerous private (or commercial) services in the Yellow Pages under "Home Health Services" or "Nursing." The family physician or staff at a hospital's social work department can probably recommend reputable ones. Also, not all those listed perform homemaking services as well as nursing ones, so call around for comparisons—and for fee comparisons as well, since these are not nonprofit companies. However, part or all of their costs will usually be covered by clients' health insurance.

Specialized Help

If your care receiver has a specific disability or condition, you may be able to get help from the organization set up to provide assistance to those with that condition.

For instance, people with Alzheimers and their caregivers can obtain counsel and advice from people with experience of the disease by contacting the local branch of the Alzheimer Society of Canada. Some branches have day programs for Alzheimers patients. Some also have home visiting programs which send a trained volunteer in to sit with your care receiver for an hour or so, freeing you up.

Other organizations that provide direct help include the Arthritis Society, the Canadian Cancer Society, the Canadian National Institute for the Blind, the Heart and Stroke Foundation of Canada, the Parkinson Foundation of Canada and the Simon Foundation for Continence Canada. The last-named provides information to those who suffer from incontinence, a loss of bladder and/or bowel control; it can be reached via a toll-free number, 1-800-265-9575.

Respite Care

Respite care programs are set up to provide caregivers with much needed relief. People caring for those with Alzheimers or other dementias especially need relief since theirs is almost a 24-hours-a-day job, but all caregivers need time off if they are to remain healthy and useful to their care receivers.

Most commonly these days, hospitals, health centres and nursing homes set aside some beds for respite care. A public health nurse or perhaps the family physician can tell you which centres to contact. If your care receiver's sojourn in a respite care bed will coincide with an event that can't be rescheduled—a vacation you have already reserved perhaps—book in for respite care well ahead if you want to be sure of getting a bed.

Probably the second most popular form of respite care involves trained people coming into the home to be with care receivers, so caregivers can have time off. Often these are trained volunteers working for the specialized organizations as noted in the previous section of this chapter.

And of course caregivers are freed up, sometimes for quite lengthy periods, when professional helpers come into the home. For instance, a Red Cross worker might come in fairly early in the morning, first to provide toast and coffee in bed for breakfast, next to help a client bathe and dress, then to help with an exercise program and finally to prepare and serve lunch. If you live in Quebec, note that some CLSCs provide respite sitters.

In Edmonton, the Capital Care Group, a nonprofit provider of services for elders, has an innovative and valuable night respite program. Three nights a week, up to four people with Alzheimers or another form of dementia are brought to a central location where, under the supervision of a nurse and between naps, they watch videos, play games, talk and snack. (People who have dementia commonly have difficulty falling asleep and staying asleep.) After being served break-fast, they go home. Since many caregivers to people with Alzheimers and other forms of dementia become worn out to the point of illness because of highly disturbed sleep, one hopes that other organizations across the country will follow Capital Care's lead and initiate night respite programs.

If you are unable to find someone to provide respite care in the home, contact your local CIC or a public health nurse to find out where to go.

Acquiring Caregiving Skills

"We believe you have to take care of yourself in order to take care of other people, and we know that caregivers quickly get burned out with their added responsibilities."

Margaret McArthur, a York Region community health nurse, is talking about a series of courses she runs called Care to the Caregiver. "We talk about anger and guilt," she says. "We give people permission to talk about these feelings that they haven't been able to share with anyone else." People respond well to the interactive style of the courses, she says. "You see these people around the table, and they bond like crazy! The second night they are together, you would swear they were all old buddies, laughing and crying together. They give each other great ideas about how to get through another day."

A public health nurse can tell you whether the local health board runs courses to help people acquire caregiver skills. Another source of education is the local family service association. Lynn Gallagher runs courses for Metro Toronto's association. Among her topics are caring for an aging parent, relative or friend, coping with caring, and workshops for people whose care receivers are about to go into permanent care and for those whose care receivers have just gone into permanent care. "I also counsel caregivers individually," she says.

Hospitals, especially those specializing in geriatric care, are another source of education. At the Baycrest Centre for Geriatric Care, Sheila Smythe's department holds workshops and arranges lectures for caregivers whose care receivers are cognitively impaired. Smythe describes her role as "offering counsel to the families of elders, finding out what's available in terms of resources, helping them tap into those resources, and dealing with a whole range of concerns about the future."

Yet another source may be your local branch of the St. John Ambulance. This organization quite often runs courses that teach people how to give care to older people who have some disability. In sum, there are many lifelines out there for caregivers. Make use of one or more and you will be doing yourself and your care receiver a favor.

CHAPTER THIRTEEN

How Are You Doing?

Toronto psychologist Dr. Pearl Karal says that, in her experience, most caregivers do an excellent job. But often they themselves don't think they do because they set standards that are too high.

"A caregiver I know feels absolutely guilty because she doesn't love her aged and very unloveable mother," Dr. Karal says. "People should set realistic expectations of themselves as caregivers. If they are making slaves of themselves, this violates their own worth as individuals. You don't have to like everybody. If you are a nurse, you don't have to like your patients, and if you are a caregiver, you don't have to like your care receiver. This doesn't mean you are not doing a good job."

Perhaps by now you are wondering what kind of a job you are doing as a caregiver. This chapter is designed to help you measure and perhaps to enhance your performance. It will help you judge whether you are trying to do too much or too little, and whether the job is having a positive or negative effect on your own life.

Rating the Quality of Your Care

Here's a self-test to help you rate the quality of care you provide In each of the five cases below, give yourself an excellent, good, fair or poor rating. If your care receiver is capable of doing the ratings, ask her or him to do so too.

SELF-TEST #6

- Personal hygiene (i.e., cleanliness, freshness) of body, skin, hair, nails
- Personal presentation: neatness, cleanliness and appropriateness of clothing and footwear
- Maintenance of living and sleeping areas
- Planning and preparation of nutritious and appealing meals
- Physical fitness: provision for and scheduling of exercise as part of the daily routine

Ratings of less than good indicate areas that merit your attention.

Moods and Feelings

Both your own moods and feelings and those of your care receiver are highly indicative of how good (or bad) your relationship is and hence how you are performing as a caregiver. Here again, both you and your care receiver should participate. Take a ruled sheet of paper, write the numbers 1 to 14 (corresponding to the statement numbers) down one side, then divide the paper into two vertical columns. Head one column "Now," the other "In the Past." As you respond to the statements enter R, O or N—for Regularly, Occasionally or Never. Comparing your and your care receiver's past and current moods and feelings will soon show you whether the situation is stable, improved or going downhill.

Note that there are no right or wrong answers on this self-test and the one that follows. The difference between what you did in the past and what you are doing now will give you some idea of the effect of caregiving on you.

SELF-TEST #7

1. I find myself humming, singing, or whistling.
2. My control over my temper is poor.
3. I feel an overall sense of contentment.
4. I feel a need to express my complaints about other people and the world in general.
5. I take changes and setbacks in my stride.
6. I find myself smiling or laughing at something or someone
7. I find myself criticizing others.
8. I experience feelings of helplessness and despair.
9. My sense of humor is good.
10. I feel I've suffered mostly losses in my life.
11. I feel appreciated and approved of by someone.
12. I have feelings of love and warmth for my family.
13. I enjoy helping others.
14. I feel trapped in the caregiver/care receiver role.

Hobbies and Interests

Here's another self-test for both you and your care receiver to do. As in the previous section, you are comparing your activities now and in the past. Clearly, a narrowing of interests and activities is not a good sign. As in the immediately previous section, take a sheet of paper, write the numbers 1 through 10 (corresponding to the activities listed) down one side, then divide the remaining space vertically, heading one column "Now" and the other "In the Past." In the space beneath these headings enter R, O or N—for Regularly, Occasionally or Never.

SELF-TEST #8

1. Visiting friends, relatives and neighbors
2. Entertaining friends, relatives and neighbors
3. Learning new ideas and skills
4. Physical activities such as sports, dancing and walking
5. Watching television or videos
6. Going to the movies and playing cards
7. Reading
8. Listening to music
9. Traveling, going on excursions and camping
10. Other (please specify)

Asking Others' Opinions

One way of measuring your success as a caregiver is to ask other people for their opinions.

Ask your care receiver—but take the response with a grain of salt unless the relationship between you is excellent and open. If you are a trifle bossy or short-tempered, your care receiver may say you are doing a terrific job in order to keep on your sunny side. On the other hand, if she or he is a cantankerous, demanding person, you may be told you're doing an inadequate job.

If a nurse and/or social worker visits your care receiver, ask for opinions from them. Granted, they don't see the two of you together all the time, but they will be able to judge from the state of your care receiver's health and mood whether this is a generally well looked after and contented person. Your care receiver may also have commented to a visitor on your performance when you were out of the room.

Ask any good friends your care receiver has. They will be able to judge whether she or he appears to be well looked after. And they are highly likely to have heard this person make comments about you.

If you have a good friend, here's the source of another opinion, and an especially valuable one if the friend is also a caregiver. (Perhaps you belong to the same support group.)

If your care receiver lives with you and other members of your family, ask those others. And observe their behavior. Are kids still bringing their friends around? If they have stopped doing so, this may be a negative sign, pointing to an atmosphere in the house that is not good.

Probably the worst person to ask "How am I doing?" is a sibling. Several people interviewed for this book say caregivers' siblings quite frequently stand back, offer no help and instead criticize the caregiver's efforts relentlessly.

When asking for opinions, if you in turn are asked questions about your behavior as a caregiver, you must of course be diplomatic but strictly honest in your replies.

Stress and Anxiety Symptoms

Our bodies give us physical symptoms as warnings that we are overstressed. And an overstressed caregiver may be doing a less than excellent job. If you have noticed any of the following signs in yourself, you should consider changing your habits.

- Sleep problems: difficulty in falling asleep, waking often, waking early and feeling anxious
- Decreased resistance to colds and other infections

- Lowered energy level, accompanied by lack of motivation, poor concentration and lack of alertness

- Lowered interest in taking proper care of physical needs, such as delaying going to the toilet

- Changed appetite: more frequent eating, eating whatever comes to hand, loss of appetite, marked changes in weight and in choices of food

- Increased need for and use of sleeping pills, alcohol, painkillers, caffeine, tranquilizers or other mood-altering substances

- Unidentified pains in shoulders, neck, back or stomach

- Frequent or severe headaches

- Breathing problems: shortness of breath, shallow or heavy breathing, holding one's breath

The following are general signs of severe anxiety:

- Unusual and recurring disturbances in digestion and elimination, such as frequent diarrhea, constipation or tension spasms in the stomach or colon

- Marked changes in sexual interest or satisfaction

- Extended periods of tension and anxiety, with little or no relief from either

Warning signs also appear in the form of any of the abusive behaviors discussed in Chapter Eleven.

As well, the following mood changes may indicate severe strain or a breakdown in the caregiver's role: unusual loss of temper, fits of weeping, brooding, thoughts of death or suicide, a flat, emotionless tone of voice.

If your care receiver is showing signs of stress, here is another indication that you may be doing a less than acceptable job. In addition to the signs listed above, look for the following:

- Unexplained tensing and stiffening when you approach
- Unexplained fear of displeasing or angering you
- Attributing to you responsibility for her or his pains, frustrations and deprivations
- "Forgetting" to recognize you as a separate person with your own priorities, needs and right to live your own life.

Good and Bad Caregiver Behavior

Being a successful caregiver emphatically does not mean martyring yourself. You have a life to live too.

If you find yourself doing more and more for your care receiver, spending more and more time with him or her, until you are finally spending time with nobody else, you are becoming a martyr to the role. In so doing, you will probably lose the support and affection of other members of your family. And when your care receiver dies, you will be utterly alone and probably unable to return to the old relationships you let wither away.

Martyrs often find themselves on an emotional seesaw. Driven by guilt, they give their care receivers more time and attention than is necessary. In short order, they become exhausted and then resentful. This resentment drives them to cut back a little on the time and attention they give their care receivers. But guilt then returns and the seesaw tips back to its original position.

Martyrs usually won't accept help. They believe nobody can do as good a job of caring for this elder. Then, ridiculously, they become angry that nobody is sharing their burden, and probably end up complaining to the very people who offered help.

If you notice that your care receiver is rapidly become more dependent on you and less willing to do jobs or perform actions you know she or he is capable of doing, this may be an indication that you are becoming a martyr and providing too much care. This can actually harm your care receiver, because you are depriving her or him of activity, stimulation and responsibility. Stand back and ask yourself how this person would manage if you were suddenly removed from the scene—to hospital after an accident, perhaps. You will probably realize she or he would manage extremely poorly. And perhaps this realization will motivate you to adjust your caregiving activities to a more reasonable level.

Martyrs often believe the caregiving role is the sole reason for their existence. If you hold this belief, ask yourself: what will I do when my care receiver is no longer here? You may have difficulty resuming old habits and hobbies, finding you have grown rusty in the interim, and discarded friends and acquaintances likely won't be beating a path to your door.

If caregiving is of necessity becoming so onerous that you have no time for yourself, seek or accept help. If you are to remain healthy and balanced, you must make time to enjoy your family and friends, to be socially active in general, to keep up your hobbies and interests and to pay attention to your own appearance. "A caregiver has to ask herself, 'What is the balance between what I can do, what this person needs, and what should I do in view of my right to live my own life?'" Dr. Karal says.

If you have difficulty with some aspect of the caregiver role, don't keep this to yourself. If you don't feel you can talk to a family member about it, your family physician may be willing to talk about it, or be able to suggest an appropriate person.

Relinquishing the Caregiver Role

If you become too exhausted to continue as the primary caregiver, do not feel ashamed. Perhaps your care receiver's condition now demands that the burden of caregiving fall on professional shoulders, either in the home or in an institution.

Or perhaps you have undergone a debilitating illness, while your care receiver's condition remains unchanged. In this case, another family member or friend will probably take over, perhaps with some help from secondary caregivers.

In case you do have to hand over the role one day, start keeping some records when you become a caregiver. Specifically, keep a record of the time you spend in giving care, and one of any expense you bear as a result of caregiving. These records will give the new caregiver a good idea of the requirements of the role.

Unless an illness suddenly takes you out of the picture, your tenure and that of the incoming caregiver should clearly overlap so that you can teach the newcomer about regular routines, medications, visits from professionals such as nurses and doctors, and so on.

If you have to abandon the caregiving role, you will almost certainly feel guilty. Try to replace guilt with the realization that change can be beneficial for your care receiver as well as for you.

And, as Dr. Karal points out, "Remember that your successor steps into a role you have created and developed. So your contribution, although no longer visible, continues."

CHAPTER FOURTEEN

Getting Peer Support

Winnipeg caregiver Pat Gray heads up the Support Group for Those Caring for Elderly Relatives. The group has some 16 members—"small enough for everybody to be able to talk and get to know one another," she observes. Almost all members are daughters of their care receivers. "I can count the men on the fingers of one hand."

One valuable function of a support group, Gray says, is "being able to say exactly what you feel. My members often say, 'This is the only place I can come and laugh about it.' It may be a kind of black humor to outsiders, but as long as the tone is kept upbeat and positive, it's a valuable way of rethinking your situation, because you explain it to other people and in so doing you explain it to yourself."

What Is a Caregiver Support Group?

Caregiver support groups are also known as self-help groups since members help both each other and themselves. They form when a number of caregivers decide to meet regularly to share their experiences of caregiving and to provide emotional support for each other. Most support groups observe confidentiality, so information shared during group meetings, no matter what its nature, is not repeated to anyone else outside meetings. Most also give all members an opportunity to contribute to the ongoing discussion.

Some support groups are totally informal with no specific topics set for meetings. The proceedings are simply general exchanges of experiences and feelings kept on track by the group's facilitator or leader. Others set topics for meetings and may invite guest speakers to address these topics, which might range from drug abuse and caregiver burn-out to guilt and nutrition for elders.

In sum, caregiver support groups provide an opportunity for care-givers to receive care from each other.

Specialized Support Groups

Some support groups have members all of whom give care to people with the same condition, be that condition Alzheimers, arthritis or whatever.

If your care receiver has a specific condition, you might choose to look for a specialized group. Other members can tell you about many of the problems you may run into due to your care receiver's disability. And they can share with you their own experiences of how best to handle specific problems. As well, others with care receivers whose condition is more advanced than that of yours will be able to tell you what to expect in the future and hence prepare you for that future.

Telephone Support

Many caregivers are housebound because their care receivers cannot be left alone and they have no backup caregivers. An alternative to support group membership for them may be a telephone network.

These come into being when individuals decide to take turns calling each other for advice and emotional support. The ideal network size is four or five people, otherwise the process may be too cumbersome and time-consuming.

A similar program has been put into place by the Family Caregivers' Network Society, which serves the Greater Victoria and surrounding area. The FCNS has trained volunteer telephone companions who give advice and support to caregivers who cannot attend support group meetings, or who are so stressed they need additional support between group meetings.

How to Find a Support Group

A public health nurse or staff at the local family services association can probably tell you about support groups in your region. (Refer back to Chapter One to find out how to contact these people.) Staff in the social work department of a hospital can also probably help, as can staff at your community information centre. (Chapter Twelve contains information on how to locate a CIC.)

If you are looking for a specialized group, the local branch of the appropriate specialized organization may be able to help. For instance, the Arthritis Society helps organize support groups for those caring for people with arthritis.

Two publications may be helpful. As already noted in Chapter Four, *Eldercare*, a newsletter for family members caring for elderly relatives, publishes useful information about caregiver support groups—and about many other topics too. An annual subscription costs $18.50 plus $1.30 GST; the address is Suite 202, 12 Donora Drive, Toronto, M4B 1B4. For those living in British Columbia, every issue of *Network News*, the newsletter of the Family Caregivers' Network Society, carries a listing of support groups in the province. There is no set price, but the FCNS gratefully accepts donations. The address is #300—857 Rupert Terrace, Victoria, V8V 3E5.

Caregivers Associations

Another way to find a support group in British Columbia and Ontario (and eventually in other regions as well, it is to be hoped) is to contact the provincial caregivers association. These associations deserve special mention because, in addition to disseminating information and acting as a focal point for caregivers, they also exist to lobby for caregivers, a highly important function in an era when changes and cuts in health care services are being widely discussed.

Patsy Schell, the energetic and enthusiastic executive director of the Caregivers Association of British Columbia, says she hopes the CABC, founded in January 1994, will serve as a role model for other provinces. "We have documented how we went about achieving a successful organization," she says. "We see a need for consumer advocacy groups to speak on behalf of family caregivers."

You can reach the CABC at #170—216 Hastings Avenue, Penticton, B.C., V2A 2V6.

In June 1995, a steering committee of the Ontario Association of Family Caregivers was set up. At time of writing, the association had not sought or received funding and had no permanent address. The contact address being used was that of perhaps the most active founding member, Dr. Geila Bar-David: 61 Marlborough Ave., Toronto, M5R 1X5.

How to Start a Support Group

"Right now I am working with a group of caregivers who have been to one of my workshops and have said they would like to have an ongoing group."

The speaker is Lynne Gallagher, who runs courses and workshops on caregiving for the Family Services Association of Metropolitan Toronto. Groups quite often come into being this way, she says.

Some people who want to start support groups put up notices in public places such as libraries, community centres and hospital waiting areas.

The family practitioner, a public health nurse, the staff at a family services association and social workers in a health centre all might be able to put you in touch with other caregivers.

If you take your care receiver to day care or respite care, talk to other caregivers bringing people in as they might be interested in joining a group. Also ask staff as they may know other caregivers you might talk to.

If you are interested in starting a specialized support group, contact the local branch of the specialized organization that exists to help people with the condition you are interested in. For instance, if you want to start an Alzheimers caregivers support group, contact the Alzheimer Society.

Helpful Information for Group Initiators and Leaders

Helping You Helps Me, by Karen Hill, revised and updated by Hector Balthazar, is a good practical guide to initiating and maintaining a group. Among topics covered are leadership, membership, fund raising and problem solving. It is available from the Canadian Council on Social Development, 441 MacLaren, 4th Floor, Ottawa, K2P 2H3, price $8.

Together We Care: An Idea Book for Caregiver Support Groups, by Barbara Gunn, is another good source of helpful information. Topics covered include finding new group members, publicity, sharing out the jobs and possible meeting topics. It is available from the Caregivers' Association of B.C., #170—216 Hastings Street, Penticton, B.C., V2A 2V6, price $5 plus $2 for handling and shipping.

CHAPTER FIFTEEN

Giving Ongoing Support

White Rock caregiver Alma Battersby is talking about a woman she knows, another caregiver. "She was changing the bed four and five times a day. He has Parkinsons. She refused to put him in a home because I think she felt this would be to reject him.

"But recently she did place him, and she told me, 'I can't believe how much better it is. He is looked after properly. I go to see him every day. We play cards, we laugh, I take him out for drives and we have a good time together now.'"

Alma believes many caregivers would benefit from having their care receivers in a home. "It's far better than this constant having to change beds and feed and toilet people. I think this destroys an awful lot of pleasant feelings. You can visit someone in a home and feel you are contributing something to this person's quality of life instead of drudgery to your own life."

The relationship between care receiver and giver may improve for another reason. The former will no longer feel guilty about being a burden.

The New Caregiver Role

When someone goes into permanent care, the caregiver will still be a caregiver, but the role changes greatly of course. If you are the person in question, one of your main tasks now is to integrate yourself into the team looking after your care receiver. You should constantly monitor your care receiver's mental and physical condition and, if you see something that disturbs you, talk to the home's staff about it. Another aspect of your new role is to communicate to staff members information they need to have about your care receiver.

And, of course, you have a new role as a visitor. And if caregiving in the past has been exhausting work, as Alma's acquaintance found, you may discover the role of visitor to be a highly enjoyable one.

Frequency of Visits

Begin as you mean to go on. In other words, don't start off by visiting every day if you know you will have to cut back to three times a week before long.

Many caregivers do visit daily for lengthy periods. Haligonian caregiver Peggy Flemming recalls her father visiting her mother twice a day to help her with lunch and dinner for 14 years until she died at the age of 89.

Some caregivers go beyond visiting. Patsy Schell of the Caregivers Association of B.C. knows people who bring their care receivers home every day, then return them to the home at night.

By all means visit daily if you enjoy doing so. But don't do it out of guilt. A nurse who spent a number of years working in a retirement home says that for the guilt-driven people who make extensive visits every day, these visits become almost their sole reason for living. So what happens when their care receivers die? "Many of the caregivers simply transfer their attentions to someone else. They start visiting another person in the home on a daily basis."

For most people, a happy medium is best. Don't visit every day from dawn to dusk, maybe because you believe you are a better care provider than the home's staff. But don't stay away for lengthy periods, perhaps because you feel guilty when you see this person in permanent care.

If you don't visit on a regular basis, let your care receiver know a day or two before a visit so that he or she will enjoy anticipating it.

Who Visits

Ideally, your care receiver should have many visitors. If you have siblings, and all of you have children old enough to visit alone, you can probably arrange for your care receiver to have a visitor every day.

If you or your siblings have young children, by all means have them visit their grandparent, especially if she or he asks to see them. Warm and caring grandparent–grandchild relationships should not be discontinued because someone has gone into permanent care.

Some homes allow visitors to bring in family pets. Ask before doing this though; some homes have resident pets and you wouldn't want to be responsible for a dog fight, for instance.

Behavior Towards Staff

Use tact in your relationships with staff at the home. If you sense something is not good—perhaps your care receiver's hair looks as though it has not been washed for a long time—don't say nothing for fear that staff will take out their anger at you through your care receiver. In fact, they will probably think either you haven't noticed the condition of this person's hair or you consider it unimportant.

But don't rage at staff or bicker with them constantly either. Take your concern to the appropriate person—the home's administrator or the head nurse perhaps. Ask politely for a few moments of this person's time. Discuss your concern calmly and in a friendly manner. If the problem is one of neglect, you might refer to the heavy burden of work the staff must bear before asking whether one person might be able to squeeze in 10 minutes or so to wash your mother's hair. If this is a good home, no one will take anything out on your mother. Staff will recognize you care and will want to do things right for you.

Drawing Up Your Care Receiver's Profile

Staff members in a permanent care facility need to know things about your care receiver if they are to have a good relationship with this person and be of maximum help.

The profile you draw up should be in written form. It should include a point-form abbreviated biography of your care receiver. In this section, make sure you mention any achievements. If staff members know your mother won all kinds of awards for baking and putting up preserves, they'll be able to mention this and congratulate her. If she is capable, she may even be invited into the kitchen to do some baking.

The other two components of the profile are a list of things your care receiver likes, and a list of dislikes.

Under "Likes" include such things as being outdoors, being addressed formally rather than casually, and spending time alone reading or watching TV. Now staff will know to take her in her wheelchair out into the garden, how to address her and not to pressure her into group activities all the time.

"Dislikes" might include mashed potatoes, being cold and heights. Now staff will know to leave a couple of boiled potatoes unmashed, to make sure this person has a cardigan at hand always and to accommodate her or him in a ground floor bedroom.

Ask the home's administrator how the profile should be dissemi-nated. Perhaps it can be pinned up on a bulletin board, or, if the home has a newsletter, it might be published in it. Either way, it serves as an introduction to your care receiver not only for staff members but for other residents too. This brings an added benefit; now your father's fellow residents will know that he once won an award for saving a dog in a burning building and plays a mean game of bridge. Far from isolating him from family by having him in per-manent care, you have in fact "grown" his family to include those who drop by to hear the story of the dog and those who are also keen bridge players.

CHAPTER SIXTEEN

Living and Dying

"Most people are really grateful for the care they are given. I have never had so many thanks in my career as I have from some of the families of palliative care patients. And I have never derived so much satisfaction from my work. We form real bonds with some of the patients and their families."

Dr. Wendy Yeomans is talking about her work as medical coordinator of the palliative care program at the Vancouver Hospital and Health Sciences Centre. She and her colleagues may work with patients and families in the palliative care unit. Or they may work with patients on the regular wards. Dr. Yeomans is also on call for the Vancouver Health Department's Hospice Program.

As she notes, palliative care and hospice programs for those with incurable conditions are becoming far more common as the population ages.

Preparing for the end of life, coping with the event of death and going through the procedures that follow a death are all activities involving you, the caregiver. If you go through the motions efficiently and in good time, some of the pain may be lifted from a sad period.

There are things you can do to ensure your care receiver's wishes are realized to the end of her or his life. For instance, you should encourage—and perhaps help—this person to draw up one or more powers of attorney and a living will. If you feel both your care receiver and you would benefit from the attentions of a team such as Dr. Yeomans', you will seek palliative care. And if you are informed in advance about the responsibilities that fall upon you when your care receiver dies, your grief will not be compounded by confusion.

This chapter will explore all these aspects of both the caregiver's and the care receiver's roles.

Powers of Attorney

A power of attorney is a legal document in which one person gives another person or persons the right to manage his or her affairs, financial and otherwise.

Giving someone power of attorney is desirable not only for older people. All adults should probably give powers of attorney to people whom they trust. If you do not give someone power of attorney, and if you become temporarily incapacitated—say, following an accident that leaves you with a head injury—your affairs are frozen until a court decides who should manage them. This decision might be a long time coming, and the procedure would likely involve stiff legal fees. Meantime, your landlord has tossed your belongings out into the street because your rent is not paid, and thousands of your dollars are lying idle because you have not renewed your guaranteed investment certificates.

Your power of attorney can be limited: this person, your attorney, has the authority to manage only a certain aspect of your affairs. Or it can be blanket: this person has the right to manage all your affairs.

It can be for a given period—maybe you are going into hospital for surgery—or for an unlimited period.

You may feel you'd like to ensure that the power of attorney comes into play only if you become incompetent, but adding a clause to this effect is not advisable. If you do so, and you do become incompetent, your attorney must prove that you are not able to manage your affairs— which will cause a delay and could involve a court appearance.

Most people give their partners power of attorney. If they are widowed, they usually give one or more of their children power of attorney. (If you give more than one person power of attorney, the document must state whether one person can act alone or whether they must agree and act together.)

If partners give each other power of attorney, they should each consider naming a second attorney. This person would then step in if both partners were rendered incapable of managing their affairs simultaneously, perhaps in a traffic accident.

If you are widowed and your affairs are highly complicated, and if you are concerned that your only child may not have the time or the expertise to manage them all during your illness, you might consider giving a financial institution power of attorney as well so that personnel there can give your child assistance as needed.

What if you and your partner have given each other powers of attorney, then you split up acrimoniously? You would revoke your power of attorney and give it to someone else you know well and trust implicitly.

Legislation governing powers of attorney (or mandates in Quebec) varies from province to province. In some cases it is quite complex. In any case, consider hiring a lawyer to draw up a power of attorney for you. The document is relatively simple, so the fee will not be high.

Your attorney should have the document. Or, if you prefer, your family physician or lawyer may keep it on file until it is needed, when it will be handed to the attorney.

If your care receiver has not already given someone—most likely you—power of attorney, encourage her or him to do so right away. And set a good example. Do likewise.

Living Wills

A living will is usually a two-part document which, like a power of attorney, comes into force only when you, if you are the one making it, are no longer capable of making decisions. Unlike a power of attorney, the decisions here are predominantly ones about health care.

One part of a living will is an instruction directive. This should be detailed and exhaustive. "No heroic measures to save my life" is too vague. For instance, you might specify that if you become severely demented, you would not want to undergo lifesaving surgery or be fed via a tube.

The other part of a living will is the proxy directive. This specifies whom you want to make decisions for you. Choose someone whom you know well and trust, and talk at length to this person about your wishes regarding various kinds of treatment you do or do not want if you become severely incapacitated, so your proxy won't one day perhaps have to guess what your wishes might be.

What if you do become severely demented and your proxy disagrees with your directive, feeling surgery would put an end to the severe pain you suffer perhaps? Your living will should specify whether you want those treating you to carry out the orders specified in your instruction directive or listen to your proxy in the event of a conflict.

Having drawn up a first draft of a living will, discuss it with your family physician—perhaps with your proxy present as well. The physician will be able to explain why you have or have not made good choices and may have suggestions for additions.

A lawyer need not be involved in drawing up a living will but you should consider consulting one. Laws governing living wills vary by province on such matters as whether or not they should be witnessed, and a lawyer can make sure your living will is legally valid.

Your wishes may change over time. For this reason, you should review a living will occasionally, and especially if your level of health alters. And of course you should change it if your proxy dies or if your proxy is your partner and you split up.

You keep the original of the living will—but not in a safety deposit box where it may lie undiscovered. Your proxy and your family physician—and your lawyer if you have involved one—should have copies.

If you know someone you trust implicitly to make decisions, your living will might consist only of a proxy directive. And if you know of nobody whom you would trust, your living will might consist only of an instruction directive.

Note that a living will is also sometimes known as a power of attorney for personal care, a health care directive, or an advance directive. In Quebec, a proxy directive is called a mandate in advance of incapacity. The person giving the mandate is the mandator and the proxy is the mandatory.

A living will may cover matters other than health care. For instance, if you are a vegetarian you might want to specify that you be fed only vegetarian dishes. If you are concerned about your safety should you become demented and violent, you might specify that you would accept physical restraints. If your care receiver is not familiar with the concept of living wills, explain the concept and encourage him or her to consider making a living will.

If you or your care receiver would like to know more about living wills and how they might be structured, obtain a copy of an excellent booklet, *Living Will*. It is by Dr. Peter Singer, associate director of the University of Toronto's Centre for Bioethics. It costs $5 (this includes tax and shipping) and can be obtained from the Centre for Bioethics, University of Toronto, 88 College Street, Toronto, M5G 1L4.

Palliative Care

Palliative care consists of relieving unpleasant symptoms such as pain, teaching family members how to do the same and making the latter days of a life as enjoyable as possible.

Many people believe palliative care is that given only to people who are imminently dying. This is not always the case. To palliate means to alleviate the symptoms of a condition, such as pain. Of the 300 or so patients seen by Vancouver Hospital's palliative care consultation service each year, about 35% are discharged home. "We have a specific discharge planning checklist," Dr. Yeomans says. Among other things, the list covers prescriptions and how to set up care in the home. "We teach family members about pain and symptom management and how to give injections if necessary. A lot of family education goes on before people are discharged."

Palliative care units in hospitals are usually pleasant places with a lounge for patients and visitors—and sometimes visiting family pets—to use, and overnight accommodation for visitors who want to be near their loved ones. The approach used in them is usually a team one. The team might comprise a physician, a nurse, a social worker, a chaplain, a dietician, a pharmacist, a physiotherapist and an occupational therapist. Most units also have volunteer workers.

In many cases, volunteers working in palliative care do follow-ups with the family after a patient has died. They may send out cards on three-, six- and nine-month anniversaries of the death, for instance, and/or telephone the survivors. If a volunteer senses from the telephone conversation that a survivor is not handling grief well, he or she may arrange for bereavement counseling from a member of the team, or alternatively recommend a community agency that does professional counseling.

Palliative care at home will be given by professionals if treatment of some kind is required. If the need is for moral support and perhaps some physical help, many hospice organizations are staffed entirely by volunteers who offer everything from respite care and light meal preparation to companionship and help with housekeeping chores. Often, the volunteers' involvement does not end with death; many organizations also offer bereavement counseling.

If you are now—or soon will be—caring for someone who is terminally ill, you would almost certainly benefit from viewing *Doing What I Can*, a sensitive and helpful video about giving palliative care. Caregivers to people who were terminally ill share their experiences with the viewer. The 30-minute video was produced and directed by Arthur Uyeyama, a video production specialist on the staff of Credit Valley Hospital. It is available from Credit Valley Hospital, Media Services, 2200 Eglinton Ave. W., Mississauga, Ont., L5M 2N1, for $12.60, a price that includes taxes and shipping and handling fees.

Canada has several hospice buildings. One such is the Dorothy Ley Hospice in Etobicoke, Ontario, which specializes in terminally ill cancer patients. Another is Casey House in Toronto whose clientele is composed entirely of AIDS patients.

Those who usually have the greatest need of palliative care are cancer patients and those with AIDS, but sometimes people with liver or kidney disease require special care.

If you believe your care receiver will need palliative care at some time in the future, Dr. Yeomans advises, "Find out as much as you can about resources available to you, and do this early before the patient needs a lot of intensive care so that there is not the stress of learning about the system while the person is symptomatic. It's a lot easier to explain the philosophy of palliative care to a person who is fairly well."

To find out what palliative or hospice care is available in your area, ask your family physician, the local public health department, staff in a hospital's social work department or your community information centre.

Last Responsibilities

If death is anticipated in the home, confirm ahead of time that the family physician will come to the home to pronounce death and provide support for the caregivers.

If an ambulance is called, attendants are legally required to attempt to resuscitate the patient until directed by a physician, which can be distressing for caregivers to witness. This situation can be avoided by having a written "no cardiopulmonary resuscitation" order signed by a physician in the home.

If your care receiver expressed a desire for a funeral, you or the family physician should call the funeral home of choice. If you wish, the funeral director will take over from here on in, arranging for necessary documentation, the religious service, automobiles, flowers and even the purchase of a cemetery plot.

Memorial societies cut down funeral costs by about half. They work through funeral homes, but embalming is not done, caskets are inexpensive and services are simple.

If your care receiver didn't want a funeral, you or the physician should still call the funeral home. It will furnish a casket and provide transportation to the cemetery or crematorium, and will handle all paperwork, for a small fee.

You and your care receiver are more fortunate than those giving and receiving care as little as 50 years ago. Today, there are new and powerful medications to combat pain. There are specialists in pain management.

More and more palliative care teams, institutions and individuals are coming into being. Today, in short, there are more and more specialists in pain and dying to help ease the transition to what in effect is the last phase of life.

Remember all this in bad times, when you can recognize nothing fortunate in either your or your care receiver's situation.

And at all times, remember that you are not alone. On your side, and wanting to help you, are all the busy caregivers, both professional and familial, who showed their desire to help by freely giving of their time and their knowledge and wisdom during the creation of this book. Join me in feeling gratitude to them. I hope their counsel has been and will continue to be of value to you in the vital caregiving role you have chosen to assume.

Take care!

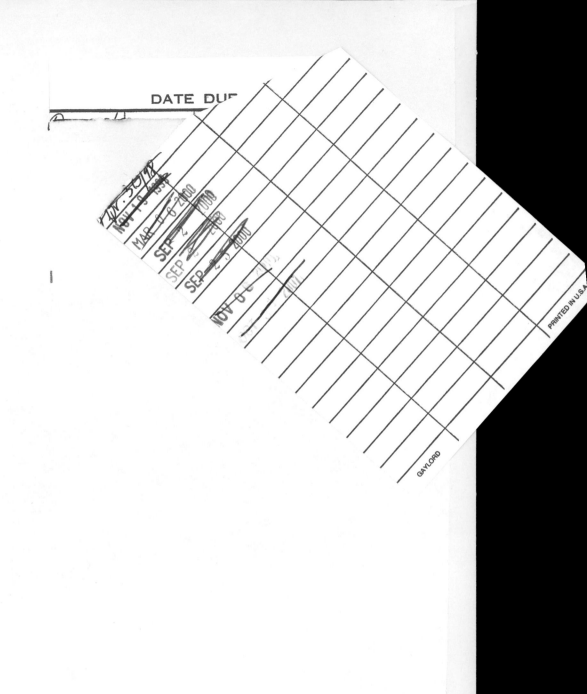

DATE DUE